NOW AND THEN

NOW
AND
THEN

Frederick Buechner

Harper & Row, Publishers, San Francisco

Cambridge, Hagerstown, New York, Philadelphia
London, Mexico City, São Paulo, Sydney

FIRST EDITION

Designer: Jim Mennick

Library of Congress Cataloging in Publication Data

Buechner, Frederick
    NOW AND THEN.

    1. Buechner, Frederick. 2. Presbyterian Church—Clergy—Biography.
3. Clergy—United States—Biography. 4. Novelists, American—20th century
—Biography. I. Title.
BX9225.B768A36 1983   285'.13[B]   82-48413
ISBN 0-06-061161-8

83 84 85 86 87 10 9 8 7 6 5 4 3 2 1

For Judy,
then and now

Contents

"We want only to show you something we have seen and to tell you something we have heard . . . that here and there in the world and now and then in ourselves is a New Creation."

—Paul Tillich, *The New Being*

Introduction

IN A BOOK called *The Sacred Journey,* I told the story of my life from its beginnings in the summer of 1926 to the point at which, some twenty-seven years later, I found myself about to enter Union Theological Seminary in New York for the by no means unwavering purpose of becoming a minister. I made no attempt in that book to tell the whole story. I left out lots of people who had been very important to me in favor of others who had never seemed especially important at all until I started thinking about them. I left out adventures I'd had. Except for occasional references, I left out pretty much the whole dimension of my life that had to do with matters like sex, money, travel, health, and, as it suddenly occurs to me now, movies, which I suspect have a great deal more to do with who we all of us are—especially those who, like me, grew up before television—than we commonly suppose. The technicolor extravaganzas and swashbuckling spectaculars of the late thirties, forties, fifties, the great World War II films, the comedies of

Laurel and Hardy, W. C. Fields, the Marx Brothers—who can measure the profound effect that, for better or worse, they had upon us all while the bloom was still on them or how differently confirmed movie-goers like me would have turned out, both as artists and as human beings, if we hadn't grown up at the time of *Les Enfants du Paradis, Rashomon, The Wizard of Oz,* and *Casablanca?* But, be all that as it may, I focused instead on those past events which, although I hadn't been aware of it at the time, I could more clearly see as having set the stage for, to have foreshadowed, my becoming a Christian and deciding to go to seminary mainly because I couldn't think of any other move dramatic and official enough to commemorate such an unexpected turn of events in my life. In the pages that follow, what I set out to do is simply to bring the story up to date. There is nothing like talking about yourself to loosen your tongue.

There is something more than a little disconcerting about writing your autobiography. When people have occasionally asked me what I was working on, I have found it impossible to tell them without an inward blush. As if anybody cares or should care. As if I myself should even care that much—like showing my baby pictures to strangers. And there is something a little geriatric about it, too —an old codger putting his affairs in order as the end approaches, marking his prized possessions so his heirs won't squabble over them later, writing names on the backs of old photographs so someday somebody will be able to tell who the people were. If anybody should ever be interested.

But I do it anyway. I do it because it seems to me that no matter who you are, and no matter how eloquent or otherwise, if you tell your own story with sufficient candor and concreteness, it will be an interesting story and in some sense a universal story. I do it also in the hope of encouraging others to do the same—at least to look back over their own lives, as I have looked back over mine, for certain themes and patterns and signals that are so easy to miss when you're caught up in the process of living them. If God speaks to us at all other than through such official channels as the Bible and the church, then I think that he speaks to us largely through what happens to us, so what I have done both in this book and in its predecessor is to listen back over what has happened to me—as I hope my readers may be moved to listen back over what has happened to them—for the sound, above all else, of his voice.

Because the word that God speaks to us is always an incarnate word—a word spelled out to us not alphabetically, in syllables, but enigmatically, in events, even in the books we read and the movies we see—the chances are we will never get it just right. We are so used to hearing what we want to hear and remaining deaf to what it would be well for us to hear that it is hard to break the habit. But if we keep our hearts and minds open as well as our ears, if we listen with patience and hope, if we remember at all deeply and honestly, then I think we come to recognize, beyond all doubt, that, however faintly we may hear him, he is indeed speaking to us, and that, however little we may understand of it, his word to each of us is both recoverable and precious beyond telling. In that sense autobiography becomes a way of praying, and a book like this, if it matters at all, matters mostly as a call to prayer.

I

New York

I ENTERED Union Theological Seminary in the fall of 1954. If anyone had told me as little as a year or so earlier that I was going to do such a thing, I would have been no less surprised than if I had been told I was going to enter the Indianapolis 500. The preceding year I had become in some sense a Christian, though the chances are I would have hesitated to put it like that, and I find something in that way of expressing it which even now makes me feel uncomfortable. "To become a Christian" sounds like an achievement, like becoming a millionaire. I thought of it rather, and think of it still, more as a lucky break, a step in the right direction. Though I was brought up in a family where church played virtually no role at all, through a series of events from childhood on I was moved, for the most part without any inkling of it, closer and closer to a feeling for that Mystery out of which the church arose in the first place until, finally, the Mystery itself came to have a face for me, and the face it came to have for me was the face of Christ. It was a slow, obscure process which I tried to describe in the earlier book, and the result of it was that I ended up being so moved by what I felt that I found it inadequate simply to keep it inside myself like a secret but had to do something about it.

I could, of course, have done no more if no less than affiliated myself in one way or another with a particular church, could have simply read books about Christianity, talked to Christian people, set out to discover something about what a Christian life is supposed to involve and then tried as best I could to live one. But, on the one hand, that didn't seem enough to me, and on the other, it seemed too much. To the degree that what I felt was so intense and dramatic that it was not unlike being in love, I had to stand up and declare myself in some intense and dramatic way. To the degree that my ignorance of Christianity was vast and comprehensive, I felt I had to learn vastly more than I could teach myself. To the degree that I felt woefully inadequate to the task of being whatever I thought a Christian was supposed to be, I needed all the help I could get. So to seminary I went.

It was a uniform to wear, a flag to raise, a comradeship of arms to draw strength from. And in view of the general direction my life had taken up to that point, it was a little crazy too. I liked that. I felt something of what Saint Francis must have felt when he decided, to everybody's astonishment, to give everything away to serve Christ's poor. I too succeeded in astonishing almost everybody including myself, but the difference was that I was no saint. I gave nothing away. I had no idea whom I was going to serve, if anybody, or in what way I was going to go about serving them. It was rather, I think, to serve myself that I went to Union. To try to fill up some of the empty places not just in my education but in myself. To draw as close as I could to what I suddenly most needed. To nurture such faith and passion and longing as I suddenly found I had.

If not a saint, who was I then all those years ago? Since my graduation from Princeton some six years earlier, I had been an English teacher and assistant housemaster at the Lawrenceville School in New Jersey and had been reasonably good at it. I had published one very successful novel and one very unsuccessful one. Twice I had been in love with girls who, mysteriously, bore the same first name and who, when I asked them to marry me, both mysteriously turned me down. I had taken a year off from Lawrenceville to write the unsuccessful second novel and spent some seven months of that year in Europe, mostly in England, where a cousin of my father's was married to Lewis Douglas, the American Ambassador. Through the Douglases, who were enormously kind to me, all sorts of heady adventures had come my way. I remember dining with just the two of them at Prince's Gate my first evening in London and having Mr. Epps, the butler, come in to announce, "Your Excellency, Mr. Churchill is on the phone." I remember meeting Princess Margaret, no taller than my shoulder and petaled like a rose, and rattling on nervously to her about some movie I had just seen, not knowing that with royalty you always wait for them to introduce the subject you will rattle on nervously about. At a great reception in Edinburgh, after Lew Douglas had been given the Freedom of the City there, I remember being mistaken by an ancient ex–Lord Provost for Douglas Fairbanks, Jr., who was also present, and being introduced by the old gentleman under that name to countless dignitaries who knew as well as I did that I was an impostor but who, like me, were too polite to say so. In Drumlanrig Castle, where we stayed with the Douglases' friends, the Duke and Duchess of Buccleuch, on the way home, I saw my first and only ghost—awoke just at dawn to find it sitting huge, white, faceless, in a wing chair facing my bed, then pulled the covers over my head and lay there sweating in a panic I can still almost recapture till the blessed sound of a vacuum cleaner somewhere else in the castle gave me courage enough to peer out and discover that, whatever it was, the thing had vanished.

To get on with my writing, I had finally settled in the little village of Great Milton near Oxford, where I ran into a professor of philosophy from Princeton named Jim Smith, who was teaching at Christ Church that year and became a good friend. With him I toured the great southern cathedrals, saw Stonehenge at midnight creaking with bats, heard Pius XII—hawk-nosed and bespectacled—celebrate mass at Saint Peter's on Christmas Eve, and had tea at the Villa I Tatti with Bernard Berenson, who, hearing that Smith was a philosopher, asked him to state his philosophy and, when Smith replied he didn't feel he could do it in a sentence, said, "Any question that can be asked in a sentence can be answered in a sentence"— which seemed to me as sonorous an inanity as I had heard up till then. In Paris I had tea with Alice B. Toklas, who had a black moustache and a white French poodle, the namesake and successor of the famous Basket she had owned with Miss Stein; and in the gardens of Versailles, in the company of one of those two girls with the same first name, I was so overwhelmed by my sense of the sadness and lostness of all that vanished glory that the tears ran down my cheeks and my companion never so much as noticed, which seemed even sadder still.

All this was in 1950. In the spring of 1953, I had left my job at Lawrenceville to be a full-time writer in New York, and it was that fall, with my third novel failing to come to life for me, that in some sense my life itself started to come to life for me—the possibility, at least, of a life in Christ, with Christ, and, on some fine day conceivably, even a life for Christ, if I could ever find out what such a life involved, could find somewhere in myself courage enough, faith enough, craziness and grace enough, to undertake the living of it. So, trailing all those clouds of glory and whatever else, I started setting forth on the daily voyage, aboard a number four Fifth Avenue bus, from my bachelor apartment on Madison Avenue at 74th Street to the seminary at Broadway and 120th.

In terms of Union's history, I couldn't have gone there at a more auspicious time. It was in its golden age. Reinhold Niebuhr was there, and Paul Tillich was there, those two great luminaries. Martin Buber came to lecture, looking like somebody out of a musical comedy with his stringy beard and a Yiddish accent so impenetrable that I found it impossible to understand more than a few words he said. Less famous but no less powerful as teachers there were, supremely, James Muilenburg in the Old Testament department, not to mention Samuel Terrien, and John Knox in the New Testament department. There was Paul Scherer to teach homiletics, Wilhelm Pauck and Cyril Richardson in Church History, and, in the Philosophy of Religion, Robert McAfee Brown, who, like me, had several nervous tics so that we used to twitch at each other across the distance between his lectern and my seat. There was New Testament Greek to learn, a different kettle of fish from the classical Greek I'd dabbled in at school and college, and Hebrew that Muilenburg daily exhorted us to dream of learning, a different kettle of fish from just about everything. There was the field work program under which you took on supervised part-time work in some church or church-related institution, and the work I chose was with the East Harlem Protestant Parish trying to find jobs mainly for blacks and Puerto Ricans, many of whom, because of the language barrier, or problems with drugs or alcohol, or lack of any kind of training, were virtually unemployable—I who had grown up among WASPs and had known blacks only as servants, who had done my senior thesis at Princeton on the function of metaphor in English poetry, and had never before had to look for a job even for myself because, as an alumnus of Lawrenceville, I had had the job there fall more or less into my lap.

College for me had been a Renaissance sampling of whatever happened to catch my fancy—medieval history and creative writing, literary criticism and American architecture, Russian and German in addition to Greek—a random accumulating of riches for no motive more far-reaching than simply to enrich myself. Seminary, on the other hand, was my Reformation. Such skills of reading, writing, understanding, as I had picked up during my disheveled and war-interrupted college career I gathered together and directed toward a more or less single end. I wanted to learn about Christ—about the Old Testament, which had been his Bible, and the New Testament, which was the Bible about him; about the history of the church, which had been founded on the faith that through him God had not only revealed his innermost nature and his purpose for the world, but had released into the world a fierce power to draw people into that nature and adapt them to that purpose, the church that not even the assorted barbarities and blunders of its ragged two thousand years had ever quite managed finally to discredit or destroy; about the theological systems that the passion of his original followers, and of Saint Paul in particular, had been distilled into. No intellectual pursuit had ever aroused in me such intense curiosity, and much more than my intellect was involved, much more than my curiosity aroused. In the unfamiliar setting of a Presbyterian church, of all places, I had been moved to astonished tears which came from so deep inside me that to this day I have never fathomed them. I wanted to learn more about the source of those tears and the object of that astonishment. I wanted to know, and be known by, people who knew greatly more about Christ than I did, were greatly closer to him than I was, greatly more aware of what they were about and of what he was about in them. Maybe above everything, I wanted to *do* something for him; and since—as writer, reader, teacher—most of my doing in the past had involved paper and pen, books and study, a seminary seemed the proper place to do it.

Part of the truth, too, I think, was that the circumscribed, academic world of the seminary seemed a safer place to start than the world itself with all its awesome needs, demands, risks. I knew that the greater world was the one where ultimately you had to be whatever a Christian was, but if that was to be my destiny at all, I thought, it would have to come later. I was not entirely sure at that point that the ministry was to be for me, but I was sure enough to give it a one-year try, and by luck I was granted for that year a Rockefeller Brothers Theological Fellowship under a program which had been dreamed up at just that time for people in just my state of indecision. I was far from sure, too, of either what becoming a Christian minister was going to cost in other than financial terms or whether I would be willing to pay that cost once I found out what it was, but with the Rockefellers behind me to finance just my brand of foot-dragging, I was eager at least to investigate the matter.

Meanwhile, the only sacrifice that seemed to be required of me was to give up my career as a writer for a time, and since that had not been going very well for me lately anyway, it was not a difficult sacrifice to make, and I was richly embarrassed by the people who took the romantic view that I had done some noble, selfless thing. The one real difficulty that my choice did involve was the suspicion that maybe in the long run I would have to give up writing for good. When Gerard Manley Hopkins decided to enter the Jesuit novitiate in 1868, he assembled all the poems he had written up to that point and burned the lot, writing to his friend Robert Bridges that he "saw they wd. interfere with my state and vocation."[1] I, on the other hand, characteristically hedged my bet. Just as I did not go live in a seminary dormitory but kept my old apartment, my old friends, more or less my old way of life, I merely set my unfinished novel aside not so much as scorched. But I think I knew what Hopkins meant. Maybe the God who offered everything, at the same time demanded everything. Maybe the day would come when I would have to renounce my dreams of literary glory forever. But what I was renouncing them for seemed to me so much more alive and immediate that, at the time, the idea of having to give them up even for good didn't seem all that painful to me. People who admired me as a writer were by and large either horrified or incredulous. Even George Buttrick, whose extraordinary sermons had played such a crucial part in my turning to Christianity, said it would be a shame to lose a good novelist for a mediocre preacher. And deep inside myself the issue was far from permanently settled either. But for the time being it seemed dim and remote compared with the new life I was entering.

In the last analysis, I have always believed, it is not so much their subjects that the great teachers teach as it is themselves. In some box in the attic, or up over the garage, I must still have notes on the lectures I heard given by Niebuhr, Tillich, and the rest of them. It would be possible to exhume them and summarize some of what struck me most. But though much of what these teachers said remains with me still and has become so much a part of my own way of thinking and speaking that often I sound like them without realizing it, it is they themselves who left the deeper mark.

I see Reinhold Niebuhr, for instance, in a beret with the wind ballooning out his raincoat as he walks his poodle along Riverside Drive. A stroke had left his speech slightly indistinct at times and one arm less than fully functional, but he always gave me the impression of great energy and wit, great involvement in the events of his time. He had been Roosevelt's adviser. He was Auden's friend. There seemed to be no phase of human history that he didn't have at his fingertips, no eminence that he couldn't have attained in any field where he'd chosen to attain it; but it was to the church that he gave himself in all its shabbiness as well as all its glory, to his students, to the work of Christ, whom he served with all his urbanity and shrewdness—that tamed cynic, as he called himself, his bad arm tucked in against his chest and his speech slurred. It was the glittering breadth of his knowledge that I remember best, his gift for applying the insights of the Christian faith to the whole spectrum of politics, economics, international affairs. He was bald, owlish-looking, with deep frown-lines, a deep-cut, sardonic mouth. He had a nose quick to sniff out the irony and ambivalence of things in general and of piety in particular, an eye sharp to perceive that the children of darkness are apt to be not only wiser but often more appealing and plausible than the children of light.

If with Niebuhr it was breadth and incisiveness, with Tillich it was depth and suggestiveness. His German accent was heavy even after years in this country—"If any-vun hass a kvestion, vill he please raise his finger" (pronounced to rhyme with *singer*)—and *crucification* was only one of the Amos-and-Andy words he occasionally used. My impression is that he mostly read his lectures with no attempt to illustrate them or dramatize them and in a vocabulary thick with multisyllabic abstractions and philosophical technicalities. But you sat there transfixed anyway. I remember hearing him lecture one winter afternoon on the subject of eternity in terms so metaphysical and abstruse that I had only the faintest idea what he was saying; but with the snow billowing past the window and the radiators hissing, I had so strong a sense of being caught up by him into eternity myself that it was like sitting there in the midst of it as I listened. I remember his insistence that before religious faith can make more than superficial sense, you have to take seriously the shattering questions arising out of human existence to which religious faith claims to have answers. I remember his view that any language you apply to God, no matter how apparently straightforward, is actually metaphorical language so that even the words *God exists* cannot be taken literally but only as a kind of poem. God does not stand out of being *(ex + sistere)* like the rest of us but is himself that out of which the possibility of being comes, or the ground of being, to clarify one metaphor by way of another.

I remember also his forging out of his strange English new ways of expressing old realities—like sin as that which increases our separation from each other, from ourselves, and from God; and the saving power of God in the world as the power to move us toward what he termed reconciliation, reunion, and resurrection and summed up as the New Being. "No particular religion matters," he said, "neither ours nor yours. But I want to tell you that something has happened that matters, something that judges you and me, your religion and my religion. A New Creation has occurred, a New Being has appeared; and we are all asked to participate in it. . . . Don't compare your religion and our religion, your rites and our rites, your prophets and our prophets. . . . All this is of no avail. We want only to show you something we have seen and to tell you something we have heard . . . that here and there in the world and now and then in ourselves is a New Creation, usually hidden, but sometimes manifest, and certainly manifest in Jesus who is called the Christ."[2]

Here and there. Now and then. Usually hidden. By laying all his erudition aside and speaking with such plainness and candor of himself, he spoke to me also of myself and pointed me to a way of speaking that I have never forgotten. I was present at the last lecture he gave at Union before his retirement. The room was unusually crowded, and when he finished speaking, everybody stood up and clapped till their palms stung. I don't remember his saying anything particular by way of acknowledgment, but when he reached the door to leave, he turned for a moment to face the applause and, with the smile of a small boy on his birthday, raised one hand to ear-level and waved his fingers at us. Pronounced to rhyme with *singers.* It was the last time I saw him.

But for me, as for most of us studying there in those days, there was no one on the faculty who left so powerful and lasting an impression as James Muilenburg. He was an angular man with thinning white hair, staring eyes, and a nose and chin which at times seemed so close to touching that they gave him the face of a good witch. In his introductory Old Testament course, the largest lecture hall that Union had was always packed to hear him. Students brought friends. Friends brought friends. People stood in the back when the chairs ran out. Up and down the whole length of the aisle he would stride as he chanted the war songs, the taunt songs, the dirges of ancient Israel. With his body stiff, his knees bent, his arms scarecrowed far to either side, he never merely taught the Old Testament but *was* the Old Testament. He would be Adam, wide-eyed and halting as he named the beasts—"You are . . . an elephant . . . a butterfly . . . an ostrich!"—or Eve, trembling and afraid in the garden of her lost innocence, would be David sobbing his great lament at the death of Saul and Jonathan, would be Moses coming down from Sinai. His face uptilted and his eyes aghast, he would be Yahweh himself, creating the heavens and the earth, and when he called out, "Let

there be *light!"* there is no way of putting it other than
to say that there would *be* light, great floods of it reflected
in the hundreds of faces watching him in that enormous
room. In more or less these words, I described him in a
novel later, and when I showed him the typescript for his
approval, he was appalled because it seemed to confirm
his terrible fear that he was making a fool of himself.
And, of course, if it hadn't been for his genius, for the
staggering sincerity of his performance, he might almost
have been right. It was a measure of folly as well as of
strength and courage, I suppose, to let himself come so
perilously close to disaster.

"Every morning when you wake up," he used to say,
"before you reaffirm your faith in the majesty of a loving
God, before you say *I believe* for another day, read the
Daily News with its record of the latest crimes and trage-
dies of mankind and then see if you can honestly say it
again." He was a fool in the sense that he didn't or
couldn't or wouldn't resolve, intellectualize, evade, the
tensions of his faith but lived those tensions out, torn
almost in two by them at times. His faith was not a
seamless garment but a ragged garment with the seams
showing, the tears showing, a garment that he clutched
about him like a man in a storm. In teaching the prophets,
he wrenched into juxtaposition faith, on the one hand, as
passion, as risk, as shuddering trust even in the face of
despair and darkness, and, on the other, as mere piety,
sentimentality, busyness. He held up Jeremiah in his cis-
tern over against the Every Member Canvass, committee-
manship, the mimeograph machine, and would prance
down the aisle parodying the cozy old Jesus hymns —
"He walks with me, and he talks with me, and he tells
me I am his own." The cluck of his laugh was always in

part a cluck at himself. The flush of his smile, with his eyes delicately lowered like a girl's and his chin tucked in, was a smile both of deprecation and self-deprecation. His prayers, he once told me, were mostly blubbering, and you felt that he prayed endlessly.

He was a fool, I suppose, in the sense that he was an intimate of the dark, yet held fast to the light as if it were something you could hold fast to; in the sense that he wore his heart on his sleeve even though it was in some ways a broken heart; in the sense that he was as absurdly himself before the packed lecture hall as he was alone in his office; a fool in the sense that he was a child in his terrible candor. A fool, in other words, for Christ. Though I was no longer at Union when he gave his final lecture there, I am told that a number of students from the Jewish seminary across the street attended it and, before entering the great room, left their shoes in the corridor outside to indicate that the ground on which they stood with him was holy ground.

In her book *Holy the Firm,* Annie Dillard writes, "The higher Christian churches . . . come at God with an unwarranted air of professionalism, with authority and pomp, as though they knew what they were doing, as though people in themselves were an appropriate set of creatures to have dealings with God. . . . If God were to blast such a congregation to bits, the congregation would be, I believe, genuinely shocked. But in the low churches you expect it any minute."[3] In that sense, I think, Muilenburg never knew what he was doing, was never a pro. But, as a scholar, he knew plenty and demanded plenty from his students. He was uncompromising in his insistence, especially, upon the necessity of exposing the Bible to all the modern instruments of literary and historical criticism and refused ever to sacrifice, or to let any of us sacrifice, scholarly integrity to the demands and presuppositions of conventional religiosity. In order to impress upon his students what he felt to be the crucial importance of this approach, he assigned us the task of writing what was known to fame as the Pentateuch Paper. In it we were to expound and support by close textual analysis the hypothesis that the first five books of the Old Testament could not be a single work written by Moses, as traditionally supposed, but were a composite work consisting of some four or more documents, each of which had its own style, theological outlook, and polemical purpose. The paper came as the climax of Muilenburg's introductory course, but the shadow it cast was a long one, and from the earliest weeks it loomed less as a paper than as a rite of passage. It had to be very long. It had to be very good. It had to hold water. And I remember still the acute apprehension with which I launched into it, the first paper I had written for anybody about anything since college. It turned out to be the opening of a door.

I had read here and there in the Bible before, the way people do — dutifully, haphazardly, far from sure either what I was looking for or what I was supposed to find. I was aware that there was said to be great treasure buried somewhere among all those unpromising, double-columned pages, but I had never had anybody point me very adequately to a place to start digging. I must have already been through a fair sampling of the Gospels, some of the psalms, some of Genesis, of Job; and though I have no specific memories of it, I remember having been moved and having sensed that there was something deeper down than I had ever gone to move me more deeply still. But it all seemed very hazy and elusive. Then, suddenly, with the monumental Pentateuch Paper to contend with, and the no-less-monumental Muilenburg to show the way, I was forced to look at it in a different light altogether. Muilenburg never expressed any doubt as to its being a holy book—a book not only rooted deep in the memories of Israel and rich with hope that the ancient promises would be fulfilled, but a book through which God himself speaks to his people—yet he maintained always that in another sense it was a book like any other book. It was no less a product of the times and of the peoples who had produced it. It presented the same kinds of difficulties, contradictions, ambiguities as any ancient document. On the one hand, it was to be read with the eye of faith and to the heart's uplifting; on the other hand, it was to be read as critically and searchingly as anything else.

It was from the Jacob narratives in Genesis that we were asked to glean evidence to support the documentary hypothesis, and in the process of doing that, I saw, I think for the first time, that holiness is not something hazy and elusive that we know apart from the earth but something we can know only as it wells up out of the earth, out of people even as clay-footed as Jacob, the trickster and crook, out of places as elemental as the river Jabbok, where he wrestled in darkness with a Stranger who was no stranger, out of events as seamy as the time he gulled his half-blind father out of Esau's blessing. "See, the smell of my son is as the smell of a field which the Lord has blessed,"[4] old Isaac says as he lays his hands upon Jacob, and there it is all in a moment: Jacob betrays his brother, dupes his father, all but chokes on his own mendacity, yet the smell of him is the smell of blessing because God, no less than Isaac, has chosen to bless him in spite of everything. Jacob reeks of holiness. His life is as dark, fertile, and holy as the earth itself. He is himself a bush that burns with everything, both fair and foul, that a man burns with. Yet he is not consumed because God out of his grace will not consume him.

What I began to see was that the Bible is not essentially, as I had always more or less supposed, a book of ethical principles, of moral exhortations, of cautionary tales about exemplary people, of uplifting thoughts—in fact, not really a religious book at all in the sense that most of the books you would be apt to find in a minister's study or reviewed in a special religion issue of the *New York Times* book section are religious. I saw it instead as a great, tattered compendium of writings, the underlying and unifying purpose of all of which is to show how God works through the Jacobs and Jabboks of history to make himself known to the world and to draw the world back to himself.

For all its vast diversity and unevenness, it is a book with a plot and a plot that can be readily stated. God makes the world in love. For one reason or another the world chooses to reject God. God will not reject the world but continues his mysterious and relentless pursuit of it to the end of time. That is what he is doing by choosing Israel to be his special people. That is what he is doing through all the passion and poetry and invective of the prophets. That is why history plays such a crucial part in the Old Testament—all those kings and renegades and battles and invasions and apostasies—because it was precisely through people like that and events like those that God was at work, as, later, in the New Testament, he was supremely at work in the person and event of

Jesus Christ. Only "*is* at work" would be the more accurate way of putting it because if there is a God who works at all, his work goes on still, of course, and at one and the same time the Biblical past not only illumines the present but becomes itself part of that present, part of our own individual pasts. Until you can read the story of Adam and Eve, of Abraham and Sarah, of David and Bathsheba, as your own story, Muilenburg said, you have not really understood it. The Bible, as he presented it, is a book finally about ourselves, our own apostasies, our own battles and blessings; and it was the discovery of that more than of the differences between the Jahwist, Elohist, Deuteronomic, and Priestly sources of the Pentateuch that constituted the real reward of writing that apocalyptic paper.

The trip from my apartment to Union took about forty-five minutes by the number four bus, and I must have needed that much time to make the transition between worlds so disparate. I read the Bible on my way with no less sense of urgency, I suspect, than my fellow passengers read the newspapers. I did the *Times* crossword. I watched the world go by. My memories of the world of seminary are vivid and alive still, whereas of the world of home that year I remember little. The friends I saw were mostly the ones I had made as a boy at school and college, and we did the same sorts of things we had always done—had dinner together, went to the movies, to cocktail parties, an occasional weekend in the country. One old friend, Peter, who had been recently married and was teaching history at Columbia, was particularly horrified at the turn my life had taken. He was a liberal in every sense, a self-proclaimed materialist, a believer in reason and the scientific method, an advocate of political and social reform; and in his view, my dalliance with religion was at best bizarre, at worst evidence that I had fallen victim to the forces of reaction. He couldn't let the subject drop but would twit me tirelessly on my folly. As he saw it, to take the Bible seriously was to espouse the same sort of narrow literalism that Clarence Darrow had discredited once and for all at the Scopes trial. To believe in God was to deny all the major advances western civilization had made since the Enlightenment and to subscribe to a world view so simplistic and primitive that a high school freshman would have no trouble debunking it. I was no good at arguing the matter with him and avoided it whenever I could, partly because I wasn't knowledgeable enough to refute his caricatures and partly because I was squeamish about putting up for debate anything in which my emotional investment was so great.

We had been friends since our days as classmates at school and college. We had loved many of the same books and movies and people, had taken many of the same courses, had caroused together, and at one point had contemplated setting down our combined wisdom in a single volume which was to consist of nothing but the words *I don't know* repeated again and again over hundreds of pages. But now one of us thought he did know, and the other thought he knew better, and though our friendship more or less survived, it did so only at the cost of our ducking this one issue that mattered so much to us both. Apart from Peter, however, my friends tended to view my new life tolerantly. If they had no very clear idea what I was up to or why, they accepted it at least as an eccentricity which in the long run probably wasn't going to do me any serious harm.

In addition to the worlds of Union and home, there was also the world of East Harlem, where, as part of the fieldwork program, I found myself running what the parish called an "employment clinic," though all it was was me sitting with a telephone and no other qualifications in a storefront office on 104th Street. I was born in New York and had lived there off and on all my life, but the New York I knew was bounded by Central Park to the west and Lexington Avenue to the east, to the north by 96th Street and to the south by Grand Central Station. Broadway theaters took me to the west side every once in a while and secondhand bookshops to the lower reaches of downtown, but by and large the city I knew was one relatively unscarred by violence, poverty, ugliness. Its heart was the square in front of the Plaza Hotel, where the golden angel leads General Sherman's horse by the bridle and the winds of spring blow through the trees at the bottom of the park as freshly and delicately as they blow anywhere. As a boy I used to wander there, sometimes walking with my cousin Tom Buechner as far up as the Metropolitan Museum, where we would make sketches of portraits in the galleries upstairs or lose ourselves in halls of Greek vases and mummies and armored knights down below. I remember coming out of the old Metropolitan Opera House one night after hearing *Rosenkavalier* with my childhood friend Jimmy Merrill and walking up Broadway in a tumble of neon-lit snow. I remember picnicking with a girl in ballet slippers and pigtails in the small park overlooking the East River at the foot of 57th Street. To this day, I cannot cross the

Henry Hudson Bridge and head down the West Side Drive, where the great liners used to dock, without a lurch of excitement in the pit of my stomach at the enormous power of life, struggle, beauty, concentrated in that extraordinary city. But East Harlem was another kind of city altogether—another kind of living, another kind of struggling, and with almost no beauty at all.

Many who happened into the storefront office on 104th Street did so simply out of curiosity. The place had something to do with the church, they knew. Maybe there would be a handout. It was a place to go anyway, different from most of the other places they went. Some of them were drunk, some glassy-eyed with drugs, but most of them, you felt, were just tired and bored with wandering the littered streets day after day to no particular purpose. There were a few chairs to sit in. In winter it was warm. Nobody tried to hustle them out unless they got obstreperous, and they rarely did. One cadaverous man, however, got very angry once. He said if I was so good at getting people jobs, why didn't I get a decent one for myself? Did anybody think I'd be piddling my time away up there in the slums if I could do any better anywhere else? The whole thing was some sort of racket, he said. I was some kind of phony. He wheeled around, looking for support that never came, and I remember his pounding my desk so hard that some papers slipped off to the floor, remember the deep, hollow notes of his rage, which he didn't have the energy to sustain for long and which, except for me, nobody else there paid much attention to. They seemed to know him. His name was George. Last names were rare in East Harlem. He quieted down eventually and showed me a tattoo on his arm that had something to do with his having been tortured once for being a Christian, he said. He looked like a man who might have been tortured once, but what it had to do with the tattoo he never made clear.

The part of his charge that stung, of course, was the part about my being a phony. I worked there only once or twice a week, and when I was through, I went back to a world that he could have known of only through the movies if, in fact, he ever had the price of a movie. Every winter there were church groups that would send to the parish boxes full of the Christmas cards they had received that year, secondhand Christmas cards with the part torn off where the messages had been. Instead of throwing them out with the garbage, they sent them to East Harlem under the assumption that the poor people who couldn't afford Christmas cards themselves would enjoy looking at them, showing them to their children, maybe even pasting them in scrapbooks. There were times when I felt that what I was doing there was in roughly the same hair-raising key.

I managed to find a few jobs for people. The non-English-speaking Puerto Ricans had the hardest time of it because in those days the state employment office wasn't set up to conduct interviews in Spanish, but I discovered somehow that the Horn and Hardart restaurant chain occasionally needed dishwashers whether they spoke English or not, and the Eagle Pencil factory, if I remember rightly, also came through from time to time. I think I may also have gotten a few boys into messenger jobs and a woman or two into a housecleaning service, but the closest I came to triumph was with a man whose first name was Fred. He was an alcoholic. He had seen better days. Years before, he said, he had studied Greek and could still recite the Greek alphabet. It was true. He recited it for me. He was a thickset man in his late fifties or early sixties, white-haired, with a blurred, intelligent face. If he had ever had a family, I don't remember his speaking of it. He seemed very much alone in the world, but without self-pity, hopeful in a sort of battered way, determined to pull himself together if he could manage it, but resolved to make the best of it even if he couldn't. He made much of the fact that he and I had the same first name. He saw it as a bond between us.

When he first arrived in the office, he was dressed like a tramp, but the parish always had a supply of cleaned and mended old clothes on hand, and by the time they had fitted him out, you might almost have guessed that he was a man who could recite the Greek alphabet. "This seeing the sick endears them to us," Hopkins wrote,[5] and for "the sick" he could as well have written "the poor." We became friends. He dropped by the office from time to time. I made a number of phone calls for him about jobs, the drinking seemed more or less under control, and eventually one of the interviews I arranged for him worked out, and he got a position as night watchman at one of the faculty residences at Union.

I didn't see him much after that. I ran into him once at the building where he worked, and there was a strangeness for us both, I think, in meeting each other so much out of our usual 104th Street context and in roles so different that East Harlem became like a secret we were keeping almost from each other. How were things going? He said they were going all right. Unless you had known, you wouldn't have guessed that his overcoat was a church handout. It was winter, and he had it buttoned up tight under his chin. His face seemed buttoned up tight too—less so as not to let the coldness in, I thought, than so as not to let some inner coldness out. Something good had started for him, but something good had also ended, if only something between us. Now that he had the job, his need for my services, such as they were, was at an end. What was left was just his need for somebody to be alone in the world with, and I didn't have the wherewithal for that. We both of us knew it. How were things going for me? I said they were going all right.

The last time I saw him I knew it was the last time although I no longer remember how I knew. It was on a windy street corner somewhere up near the seminary. Had he started drinking again? Had he lost his job? Was he going away somewhere, or was I? I remember only that he had to hold his hat by the brim to keep it from blowing off and that for some forgotten reason we were saying a final good-bye. I remember that I said, "I'll be seeing you," but that I knew it was not true. I would not be seeing him.

When you find something in a human face that calls out to you, not just for help but in some sense for yourself, how far do you go in answering that call, how far *can* you go, seeing that you have your own life to get on with as much as he has his? As for me, I went as far as that windy street corner up around 120th Street and Broadway, and I can see him standing there as in some way he is standing there still, and as I also am standing there still. He is alone and making the best of it with his thin, church-rummage overcoat flapping around his legs. His one free hand is raised in the air to wave good-bye. It was the last time. "Here and there in the world and now and then in ourselves," Tillich said, "is a New Creation." This side of glory, maybe that is the best we can hope for.

So we were essentially dilettantes, I and the other students who worked part-time in the East Harlem Protestant Parish, up-and-coming dabblers in the down-and-out. We came, and we left, and in the end we left for good and were glad to. But there were others, the regular parish staff, who gave their lives to it. They didn't just work with the poor. They lived with them. They made their homes in the same kind of tenements. They ate the same kind of food. They raised their children there and sent them to the same schools. Their backgrounds were more or less what mine had been. They were educated, resourceful, attractive people, who, you felt, if success had been what they were after, could have been successful virtually anywhere. But they had put this all behind them for a life whose rewards seemed to me as inward and obscure as its penalties seemed blatant and grim. I am sure that their motives were as mixed as anybody else's and that they were as full of shadows as the rest of us. There were times when you couldn't escape the feeling that, no matter how hard they fought against it, they thought of themselves as a kind of spiritual elite and of all other types of Christian service as comparatively irrelevant. There were times when their lightness of heart seemed forced and artificial and when their total immersion in the life of the ghetto seemed to border on the perverse. There were occasional glimpses of bitterness, envy, dissemblance among them, and some of them obviously rang truer than others. But be that all as it may, they nevertheless seemed, at their best, closer to being saints than any other people I had ever come across; and the quality of their saintness, the face it wore, the effect it produced, struck me as revealing something not only about themselves but about Christ, whose saints they were.

They had caught something from him, I thought. Something of who he was and is flickered out through who they were. It is not easy to describe. It was compassion without sentimentality as much as anything else, I think—a lucid, cool, grave compassion. If it had a color, it would be a pale, northern blue. They never seemed to romanticize the junkies and winos and deadbeats and losers they worked among, and they never seemed to let pity or empathy distort the clarity with which they saw them for no more if no less than what they were. Insofar as they were able to approach loving them, I got the impression that they did so not just in spite of everything about them that was neither lovely nor lovable but right in the thick of it. There was a kind of sad gaiety about the way they went about their work. The sadness stemmed, I suppose, from the hopelessness of their task —the problems were so vast, their resources for dealing with them were so meager—and the gaiety from a hope beyond hope that, in the long run if not the short, all would in some holy and unimaginable way be well. If, as I suspect, they looked at me and at the others who worked there only part-time as less committed than they, farther away from where the real battle was being fought, then I can say only that, of course, they were right. But they seemed less to hold the difference against us than simply to mark it and leave it for us to come to terms with as best we could.

What they make me think of, looking back, is the passage in Mark where Jesus tells the rich young ruler that if he really wants to be perfect, then he must sell everything he has and give it to the poor, whereupon what the rich young ruler does is turn on his heel and walk sorrowfully away because he has great possessions. Jesus made no attempt to hold him there, shouted no reproaches or entreaties after him, simply let him go as the parish let me go, but you feel that the look in his eye as he watched him disappearing down the road was as full of compassion for the young man himself as for the poor whom the young man could not bring himself to serve fully.[6] And they make me think, too, of how, in the same passage, Jesus bridles at the rich young ruler's addressing him as "good Teacher." "No one is good but God alone," Jesus says, and surely that is what the parish staff would I think have said too. At their strongest and saintliest, I believe, they knew that in the last analysis they weren't really a spiritual elite, not really better than other people. They were just luckier.

In any case, theirs was a road I did not take because I did not have either the stomach for it or the gift for it, but like other untaken roads, it haunts me still, leaving me with this sense that old Fred, my friend, still stands there on his windy corner and that I stand there still myself. On the road that I took instead, have I ever done anything or been anything to match in its own half-hearted and fragmentary way their degree of self-sacrifice? I genuinely don't know and feel sure that I'm better off not knowing. If I have, then it was by grace alone. If I have not, then I can only hope that at the end of the journey, where all roads finally meet, grace may prove sufficient.

The Rockefeller Brothers fellowship was only for a single year, at the end of which you were supposed to have made up your mind about the ministry one way or

the other, and as soon as you made it up either way, they
were no longer, at least in a monetary way, interested in
you. I have always found it endearing to think of those
great, hard-driving philanthropists—so above all else de-
cisive themselves—willing to finance as much as twelve
full months of indecision. In my case, it lasted longer than
that. At the end of the year, I knew I had been hooked.
I had never spent a richer year anywhere, never been so
close to total involvement in anything else I had done.
Whatever road I ended up taking, I could not imagine
leaving all that behind. But, at the same time, there was
the novel that I had put aside, a handful of half-born
characters, a story that I had only begun to tell and that
seemed all the more promising as I thought about making room in it for some of the new things I had learned,
some of the new people I had met.

And, of course, there was the world calling me too.
Dreams of fame and fortune die hard if they ever die at
all. After the bonfire of 1868, even Father Hopkins
picked up his pen again. So the question was whether to
return to Union in the fall or to take the year off to write
the novel and maybe get so caught up in the literary tide
of things that I would never return at all. It seemed very
much an either/or matter to me then. Either I was to be
a writer, or I was to be a minister. With the kind of
ministry I had observed in East Harlem in mind, I don't
think it occurred to me then that conceivably you could
be both. And in terms of that kind of ministry, of course
you couldn't.

Most of the major decisions of my life I find very hard
to remember, largely, I think, because they either more
or less made themselves or were made by me at a level
so subterranean that I can take neither blame nor credit

for them, but I can still remember anguishing my way through this one. I went to Dr. Muilenburg for advice. I consulted my friends. I knew that Christians were supposed to pray for guidance, and I tried my hand at that too, in the dark of night, in my bed at 929 Madison Avenue. The anguish was real enough, but I remember that, even at the time, the prayers seemed self-conscious and stagey. I was less a man praying than a man *being* a man praying, and no clear answer came, none that I could hear anyway, and maybe that in itself was the answer: that there was no clear right, no clear wrong, but that whichever way I chose, I would have to make it right, both for me and for the one I prayed to. It was for me to decide, and what I ended up deciding was, characteristically, to have my cake and eat it, too. I would take the year off and write a book. Then I would go back to Union and become a minister. Whatever becoming a minister was to mean.

How much do you put into an account like this? What do you put in? How differently your life sounds, feels, tastes, when you are living it from the way it sounds when you write it down with all the day-to-dayness of it forgotten or left out. On paper it sounds as if you knew where you were going and why you were going there and kept at it. It sounds as if you had a plan in mind and that one move followed another move more or less in order. It sounds as if your days were all of a piece and made sense. "That we may hereafter live a godly, righteous, and sober life" is the final petition of the prayer of general confession in the Book of Common Prayer, and you might think from this record that, after a year at theological seminary, I had made significant strides in that direction. But the truth of the matter is that I was not noticeably much godlier than I had ever been, was far from certain even what righteousness was, and was by no means either always sober or even particularly interested in being. In other words, the year off from Union was both more and less than I bargained for as years almost always are. During the course of it, I fell in love. I got married. I spent four months in Europe. Through my young wife I picked up a whole new family to have and to hold, to rejoice in and do battle with, a whole new world in which to live and move and have my being. Perhaps a few disconnected paragraphs are the best way for suggesting the random reality of the months that elapsed between my leaving Union in June of 1955 and my return to it the September of the following year.

I had never been much of a dancer—despite Miss Bloss's classes at the Plaza when I was thirteen or so, I had never mastered more than a rather eschatological box-step —and avoided dances whenever I could. But I was persuaded to go to one the spring I left Union because the people who were giving it were old friends of my family, and one of my uncles said that if I would go, he and his wife would personally undertake both to drive me there and to drive me back. He said it would do me good. So, such as I was, and hoping that my memories of Miss Bloss would see me through yet again, I went. How my life would have turned out differently if I had not gone, I can neither imagine nor want to.

Through a pair of sliding glass doors a girl came in. She was wearing a white dress. Her name was Judith. She was twenty-two, and I was twenty-nine, and not only had our parents been friends through having spent summers near each other in Quogue, Long Island, during the late twenties and thirties, but even our grandparents, all four sets of them, had had at least a nodding acquaintance. I had met her several times before, but it was only when she came through those glass doors that I actually saw her. She was slender. She was nearly as tall as I was. She loved horses and the out-of-doors. Her face looked full of light. Beyond that I will say only, with John Donne, that "all measure, and all language, I should passe,/ Should I tell what a miracle she was."[7] We were married the following spring by Dr. Muilenburg, whose hands trembled so as he read the service that we felt almost supernaturally calm by comparison.

I know several thoughtful and highly principled young couples living together without benefit of clergy or of anybody else who argue eloquently against the institution of marriage. "As long as ye both shall live" is transformed into "As long as you both shall love," and their view seems to be that to institutionalize such a relationship as theirs is to rob it of much that is most authentic and spontaneous and human about it. They point out that for a man and woman to commit themselves legally to honor and cherish each other for the rest of their lives is unrealistic at best and hypocritical at worst. Their love for each other should be bond enough to hold them together, and when the love ends, then the bond should end with it, and they should go their separate ways.

As for me, I find much in this that is persuasive. Who can deny that many a man and woman have married for no motive more edifying than that it was the only respectable way to enter into a full sexual relationship and that, as things turned out, they would have done better in every sense that one can imagine mattering much either to themselves or to God simply to have had the relationship and forgotten about the respectability which, once the first, careless rapture was passed, became a cheerless if respectable prison to them both? Who would argue that the vows exchanged at weddings are anything other than wild and improbable? Who can look at the apparent devotion and well-being of many an unmarried pair who live together, even have children together, and call them simply wrong in either religious terms or any other?

All I can say in response is that it was within the bonds of marriage that I, for one, found a greater freedom to be and to become and to share myself than I can imagine ever having found in any other kind of relationship, and that—absurdly hopeful and poorly understood and profoundly unrealistic as the commitment was that the girl in the white dress and I made to each other in the presence, we hoped, not only of most of the people we loved best in the world, but of God as well, in whose name Dr. Muilenburg somewhat shakily blessed us—my life would have been incalculably diminished without it. In any case, after two months near Oxford, in England, and two more near Innsbruck, in Austria, during which my wife wrote thank-you letters for wedding presents and I wrote a long-out-of-print novel for posterity, we returned to New York, where I completed the two further years at Union which were required for the Bachelor of Divinity degree and spent the summer in between studying Hebrew at Princeton Seminary because Muilenburg said that when God proclaimed, "Let there be light!" Hebrew was unquestionably the language he proclaimed it in. And as far as I was concerned, he was unquestionably right.

For lack of a better title, I called the novel *The Return of Ansel Gibbs.* I put Dr. Muilenburg in it, and though he was devastated at first by the idea that I had revealed to the world the fool that he feared he was continually making of himself in his marvelous lectures—"What will *Albright* say?" I remember him groaning—he was eventually reassured by his colleague John Bennett, to whom we submitted the typescript, that his fears were groundless, and our friendship was never in jeopardy. I also put a little of East Harlem in it and, in the character of Gibbs himself, something of the personality of my old Lawrenceville headmaster, Alan Heely, and of the world of government and diplomacy that I had glimpsed through Lewis Douglas. For the first time in print, I also touched, though in considerably fictionalized terms, upon my father's suicide some twenty years earlier.

Looking back at those pages now, I am surprised by how many sad memories of him I disguised a little and put into them—the failures, the moving from job to job, the note he left on the last page of *Gone with the Wind*, which came out the year he died. "He was a fine swimmer and dancer and was at home everywhere," I had one of my characters say of him. "But he had no private home inside of himself, if you understand me. . . . So when troubles forced him home, there was nowhere to go because he didn't have any home. Or if he ever had had, he'd forgotten his way there. I think he died of astonishment as much as anything."[8] I wish I had written "of homesickness" instead, but even as it stands it was perhaps a part, at least, of the truth. And yet, if I remember the writing of that book at all accurately, I am even more surprised by how little pain it cost me to set those memories down. It was as if, even after all that time, the shock of his death remained such that I still had not felt the real impact of it, still had not come to terms enough with who he had been, and who he had been to me, to be able to mourn him properly. And maybe that is part of why when my wife's father died the year after we were married, I suspect that at least some of the tears I wept over him had been some twenty years keeping.

George Merck was a great, tall circus of a man with blond hair and blue eyes who loved good food, good drink, good friends. Gene Tunney was one of his friends, and so was the novelist John Marquand, and many years before, when they were both young men at Quogue, my father had been another. When he went to restaurants, waiters clustered around him, enraptured by his rapture. He towered above everybody like a maypole, and wherever he was was a party. He had his picture on the cover of *Time.* His closet was ablaze with the hoods of his honorary doctorates. He was a tycoon. But unlike most tycoons I have run into, he was never cut off, hemmed in, by it all. New York taxi drivers and Vermont farmers, Nobel-prize-winning scientists and footloose German cousins—there was nobody who didn't interest him. He plied them with questions about the details of their lives, and when they answered him, he gave the impression that there was no life, including his own, that interested him more. I remember one spring afternoon at his house in New Jersey when suddenly—after a great *maibowle* that he had concocted himself with strawberries and white wine and the little herb *waldmeister* that he claimed made all the difference—he took me by the hand and went gamboling down a sunlit slope of green lawn, all six feet five inches of him, with me careening along beside him like a toy on a string; and for months after his unexpected death early one November morning in 1957, each time I thought of him was as if he had suddenly taken me by the hand again, and each time it nearly broke my heart.

Then that next winter, the last one that Judy and I spent in New York while I was finishing up at Union, my grandmother Buechner also died, that holy old terror with her relentless demands for love and attention from us all, that scourge of her daughters-in-law, my fierce, fast friend. She was eighty-four years old and greatly overweight. She was in the hospital with a broken hip and never to walk again. After they had operated on her and I went to see her piled high on her bed like pastry, she told me that she had had dreams that cannibals were chasing her. Then "I'm sorry I pulled through," she said. "It would have been such an easy way to slip off into oblivion." And of course she was right, and she slipped off into oblivion soon enough, or whatever it is we slip off into; and if the cannibals pursued her even there, I'm sure she gave them a good run for their money. There was no funeral because she had always been as leery of funerals as she was leery of the churches they took place in, but only a burial service, the first I ever conducted, to put her ashes near my father's and his brother Tom's and my grandfather's in Greenwood cemetery in Brooklyn, where she had been born. Stouter even than my grandmother, her youngest sister, known as Aunt Budlein, was there, leaning on a cane; and I remember how after I had finished, she turned with her great face bathed in tears and said, "Well, that is that," then went stumping off among the familiar graves. And that was that. Unlike my father-in-law's death, hers came at so much the time when she was ready for it to come that it did not break my heart, but it is certain that it broke something. It broke a tie with my childhood and with my father. It broke off part of home.

That spring, on the first of June, 1958, I was ordained in the chapel of the Madison Avenue Presbyterian Church, where some four and a half years earlier I had heard George Buttrick give the sermons that had started me on my way. I sat by myself in the front pew feeling awkward and unreal. Dr. Muilenburg preached on Elijah's handing his mantle over to Elisha. Dr. John Knox preached on two texts from Matthew. In one of them, Jesus commanded his disciples to go out into the world and proclaim the Gospel, Dr. Knox said, but in the other he told them that it would be better to have a millstone fastened around their necks and be drowned in the depths of the sea than to cause anyone who believed in him to sin. As I knelt there in the chancel with the hands of all the assembled ministers and elders heavy on my skull, I had no doubts, if I had ever had any before, that it was a risky as well as a holy trade that I had chosen.

II

Exeter

TO BE A minister, I had always assumed, meant inevitably to have a church. It meant conducting not just the services on Sundays, but the baptisms, the weddings, the funerals on whatever days they happened to turn up. It meant presiding over Sunday School and youth fellowships and other such groups whose names struck me as equally unappetizing. The word *fellowship* conjured up, for me, something on the order of a Shriners' convention, and having never been to Sunday School myself, I tended to think of it as something that any enterprising child would try to squirm out of if he possibly could. Having a church meant calling on sick people in hospitals and on the old, the lonely, the house-bound who had no one else much to call on them. It meant worrying about budgets and fund drives, committees and trustees. It meant, in short, entering a whole new world which, even after three years of preparing for it, I knew little about except at second hand, and which involved much that I not only found forbidding but felt I probably wouldn't be much good at either. I had never taken part in the ongoing life of a church before I entered seminary, and since then my job at East Harlem had smacked more of social service than of anything else. Nevertheless, what I wanted above all else was to try to bring the Christian faith to life in all its richness and depth for others the way people like Buttrick, Muilenburg, Tillich, and the rest had brought it to life for me, and for that reason what I needed more than anything else, I thought, was a pulpit. So if I could find a church that would have me, that was where I was prepared to go. As graduation from Union approached, I can't remember having even imagined any other possibility.

But then I had a letter that changed everything. It came from a man in his seventies named Robert Russell Wicks, who had been Dean of the Chapel at Princeton during my first years there, and although as a non-chapel-goer, I had never run into him then, I came to know him later when we were both teaching at Lawrenceville. While I was getting ready to leave Union, he was living in New Hampshire, where he was trying to organize a full religion program at Phillips Exeter Academy. The only religious instruction that Exeter was then offering was the one small class of seniors that Dean Wicks himself had time to teach as school minister, but he had persuaded the administration that this ought to be considerably expanded and that for that purpose they should hire somebody else to start a regular department of religion. With my teaching experience behind me and the Union diploma all but in my pocket, he wrote that he thought the job was, if not exactly a call from on high, at least a striking facsimile. Would I consider it?

I considered it. When I had left Lawrenceville some

five years earlier, I thought I had left prep school teaching for good. I had very much enjoyed my life there in most ways— enjoyed my classes especially, the Monday night revels with my English department colleagues, the long vacations to write and recuperate in—but the world of boarding school seemed too small, too comfortable, too all-absorbing, and that was largely why I left it. Exeter, it seemed to me, promised to be something else again. For one thing I was married now and thus would have a world of my own, apart from the school world, to keep me in touch with the diversity and reality of things. And in addition to that, it was clear that my role would be very different from what it had been at Lawrenceville.

Much as I had enjoyed teaching my students there how to read such classroom staples as *Macbeth, Ethan Frome, The Red Badge of Courage,* and how to write the English language with some measure of clarity and skill, it seemed to me in the last analysis to be icing on the cake. A boy could learn all I knew about reading and writing and still have little understanding of himself or his own life, have nothing to hold on to, to believe in, when the chips were down. As far as the decision for or against belief in God was concerned, most of the time he had little idea even what the issues were because no one had ever made the effort to discuss them with him. If he rejected Christianity, it was usually such a caricature of it that I would have rejected it myself, and if he accepted it, the chances were he knew equally little about what he was accepting. Compared to the teaching of other subjects, the teaching of religion at most schools I had any knowledge of tended to be cursory—a course that met only once a week for half a year, say, usually with very little work required in it and taught by people from other departments who had no real training in the area themselves. The very fact that it was relegated to such an obscure corner of the curriculum was itself, of course, a way of telling students that it was not a subject that much mattered. At Exeter, on the other hand, I would have the chance to set up some rigorous, academically respectable courses in the subject and to try to establish them as an enterprise no less serious, relevant, and demanding than the study of American history or physics. Even though it was not a form of ministry that I had ever considered, I decided to give it a try.

Therefore, according to Presbyterian usage in those days, I was ordained not as the minister of a church but as a minister without pastoral charge, or evangelist. There was a time when the word *evangelist* would have caused me as much trouble as the word *fellowship*, conjuring up Billy Sunday, Aimee Semple McPherson, and the sawdust trail, but I'd had enough Greek to know that what it meant was "bearer of good news," and that seemed fair enough. So in September of 1958 we moved up to Exeter with Judy expecting her first child that winter and with me having no clear idea what to expect at all. All told, we were there for nine years with one year's leave of absence tucked in the middle, and by the time we left, the religion department had grown from only one full-time teacher, namely myself, and about twenty students, to four teachers and something in the neighborhood, as I remember, of three hundred students or more. As far as I can see, this came about at least as much in spite of me as because of me, and at least one of the factors that helped it come about was one that might more readily have been expected to spell its doom.

The late fifties at Exeter were the period of the *nego,*

and a nego, in Exeter parlance, was a student who was negative, against, anti, just about everything. First and foremost, he was anti-Exeter itself. The faculty he saw as composed almost entirely of boors and sadists and the administration as hopelessly inept. The classes were a crashing bore. The New Hampshire climate was unspeakable and the lovely old town a bad joke. Beyond that, negos were anti-government, anti-establishment, anti-God, and anti-authority in any form whatsoever. As intellectuals, their heroes, if they admitted to having any, were people like Jack Kerouac, Allen Ginsberg, Jules Feiffer, Bertrand Russell, Sartre, and Ayn Rand. As card-carrying atheists, almost to a man, they saw religion in general, much the way my old friend Peter had, as a holdover from the dark past and a roadblock to any hope there might be for a bright future. When it came to the Christian church in particular, and more particularly still when it came to the school church, which, whether they believed in God or didn't, all students were required to attend on Sundays unless they chose a town church instead, their opposition was boundless and impassioned. It was the final outrage perpetrated upon them by the combined authority of school, parents, establishment, and the very God they wouldn't touch with a ten-foot pole even if it could be proved to them that he existed. Therefore, since Dean Wicks, as school minister, was old enough to be their grandfather and so full of benevolence and warmth and canny wit that it made it hard for them to attack him very satisfactorily, they turned instead to the young greenhorn who had been dragged in to be his sidekick. But in order to attack me properly, they had to take my courses, and thus it was that almost from the beginning I had as my students, in increasing numbers over the years, those very negos who, as the brightest boys in the school and the leaders of the opposition, both tended to set the fashion and were just what my newly hatched department needed to give it academic credibility. It was a victory which was mine without my having to lift a finger to win it.

But to win a victory, even a significant one, is not to win the war, and the war I fought was to convince as many as I could that religious faith, even if they chose to have none of it, was not as bankrupt and banal and easily disposable as they most of them believed. It was a war to prove not just to my students but to certain equally skeptical members of the faculty and administration that religion both could and should be taught at all. The feeling in both camps was that any such course, when taught by a minister, would almost surely be so biased that there would be no place in it for a dispassionate exchange of views as in other courses, but that answers would be taught along with questions as in a catechism class and that anybody who strayed from the party line would be appropriately penalized. Among certain of my older colleagues especially, there was the feeling also, I think, that religion, like sex, was indeed an important subject but that, like sex again, it was something that a boy did better to find out about on his own than to have somebody stand up at a blackboard and explain to him. It was apparent also that some of them were afraid that if too many boys decided to study religion, it would be a bad thing both for the boys themselves, who would gain more from studying some more down-to-earth subject, and for the other departments whose enrollment figures would be threatened. In other words, it was a battle that had to be fought on several fronts at once, and what gave me such a feeling of being embattled was that not just my subject was on the firing line, but I was on it myself. What those extremely intelligent, articulate, sophisticated young people were there to take potshots at were not just the religious ideas that I offered to their scrutiny, but my own recently acquired and little understood faith which was much of what gave meaning and purpose and richness to my life.

Extremely intelligent, articulate, sophisticated—they were not all of them that, needless to say, and, underneath, even the ones who were, even the most hard-bitten negos, were many other things besides. They were as full of doubts as to who they were and what they believed in as the rest of humankind. They were vulnerable on as many fronts. They felt in as many ways lost and bewildered. They were as hungry for something to enrich their lives with meaning and purpose, for something to worship even, as the very passion with which they rebelled against everything that claimed but failed to fill that hunger bore witness. And in all those ways, young as they were, they were very much like all the other people whom over the years I have tried to talk to, or write for, about the Christian faith ever since, including, God knows, myself. Negos or straight arrows, religious or unreligious, sophisticated or unsophisticated, in one form or another we all of us share the same dark doubts, the same wild hopes, and what little by little I learned from those years at Exeter was that unless those who proclaim the Gospel acknowledge honestly that darkness and speak bravely to the wildness of those hopes, they might as well save their breath for all the lasting difference their proclaiming will make to anybody.

What I also came more and more to realize was the

urgency of what I was about. The strongest argument I could make for required church was the purely practical one that even though the idea of it offended me little less than it did its opponents, I preferred to get the chance to preach to students against their will rather than never to get the chance at all. And it was the same thing with my classes although they were elective rather than mandatory. In the pulpit and the classroom both, I felt that it might well be the last chance anybody would ever have again to speak to them seriously, and in something like their own language, and at a time in their lives when they still might just be able to hear—about God and what belief in God involves and what disbelief involves too. Remembering what Dr. Knox had said about the millstone, and knowing that my students would get me even if the depths of the sea didn't, I only hoped I had it more or less straight. For nine years, therefore, I ran scared, and though that didn't make for a very relaxing time, I believe that it is the only way for people in such a job to run. If they are not scared, the chances are they know even less what they're doing than I did.

I was ordained as an evangelist, but *apologist,* I suppose, would have been, and continues to be, the more appropriate word. My job, as I saw it, was to defend the Christian faith against its "cultured despisers," to use Schleiermacher's phrase. To put it more positively, it was to present the faith as appealingly, honestly, relevantly and skillfully as I could. In this sense my more skeptical faculty colleagues were of course justified in suspecting my lack of objectivity. The deck I used was as stacked as the deck of any teachers who want their students to catch fire from whatever subject they are teaching. Tillich,

Barth, C. S. Lewis—I had my students read the most provocative and persuasive theologians I knew. And on the grounds that, even in the hands of masters, such ideas as sin and salvation, judgment and grace, tend, as ideas, to sound cerebral and remote, I tried to put flesh on the theological bones by having them read also works of fiction and drama where those same ideas appear in human form—where grace, for instance, is the power by which Graham Greene's whiskey priest becomes a kind of saint despite all his shortcomings and seedy ineffectuality; where King Lear is saved in the sense of being made aware of the poor, naked wretches of the world, made compassionate, alive, and human at last through his sufferings on the stormy heath; where sin more than Smerdyakov's villainy is what destroys the father of the brothers Karamazov as a human being, that old buffoon estranged by his own self-loathing not just from his sons but from everybody else including both himself and God. Koestler's *Darkness at Noon,* Miller's *Death of a Salesman,* Joyce's *Portrait of the Artist as a Young Man,* Lagerkvist's *Barabbas*—they were so bright and so verbal, most of those boys, that there was almost no reading that I couldn't assign them. My frustration was, rather, in discovering that although many modern writers have succeeded in exploring the depths of human darkness and despair and alienation in a world where God seems largely absent, there are relatively few who have tried to tackle the reality of whatever salvation means, the experience of Tillich's New Being whereby, even in the depths, we are touched here and there by a power beyond power to heal and make whole. Sin is easier to write about than grace, I suppose, because the territory is so familiar and because, too, it is of the nature of grace, when we receive it, to turn our eyes not inward, where most often writers' eyes turn, but outward, where there is a whole world of needs to serve far greater than the need simply for another book. I was too occupied with my job to think much about the next novel I myself might write, but it occurred to me that, if and when the time ever came, it would be the presence of God rather than his absence that I would write about, of death and dark and despair as not the last reality but only the next to the last.

I stacked the deck in favor of what I believed in, to be sure, but the game wasn't entirely fixed. I had my students read spokesmen for the other side too. Atheists were what most of them thought of themselves as being, but their seventeen-, eighteen-, nineteen-year-old atheism was apt to be as superficial and threadbare as the form of Christianity that they had abandoned in its favor. Their atheism was a denial less of God, it seemed to me, than of people telling them what to do and what to think and who to be. To get rid of God seemed to them like getting rid of required church, like finally getting out of Exeter once and for all and going on to college where the sky was the limit and there were no holds barred. So I had them read from the great existentialist atheists too, some of whom were their heroes already, and who, unlike themselves, did no dance on the grave of God, but whose voices, even at their most strident, were often full of mourning. "The existentialist," says Jean-Paul Sartre in one of the essays I assigned, "finds it extremely embarrassing that God does not exist, for there disappears with Him all possibility of finding values in an intelligible heaven. . . . Everything is indeed permitted if God does not exist, and man is in consequence forlorn, for he cannot find anything to depend upon either within or outside himself. . . . We are left alone, without excuse. That is what I mean when I say that man is condemned to be free."[9]

They also read Camus' *The Myth of Sisyphus* with its dismissal of religious faith as "philosophical suicide" and its theory of the absurd as the product of man's endless longing for the world to make sense in confrontation with the world's endless refusal to do so. "The absurd man," Camus writes, "thus catches sight of a burning and frigid, transparent and limited universe in which nothing is possible but everything is given, and beyond which all is collapse and nothingness. He can then decide to accept such a universe and draw from it his strength, his refusal to hope, and the unyielding evidence of a life without consolation."[10]

What I tried to do was let these writers speak for themselves out of their own extraordinary courage, concern, and honesty, and, for all my deck-stacking, to leave open to my students—as, if we are honest, it must always remain open to us as well—the possibility that just maybe Camus and Sartre were right. I tried to show, too, that even if they were not right, any form of religious faith or of atheism which does not take their dark and searching vision into full account is apt to be a very frail and shallow business by comparison. "What no person has a right to is to delude others into the belief that faith is something of no great significance, or that it is an easy matter, whereas it is the greatest and most difficult of all things," wrote Søren Kierkegaard,[11] and of course my students read Kierkegaard, too, as one, not unlike my old teacher James Muilenburg, whose faith existed in constant tension with his doubt, and who had seen all the darkness that Camus and Sartre were to see after him, but was never quite blinded by it to the presence, beyond it and deep within it, of unutterable light.

Finally, in this account of those long-ago classes from which I suspect I learned considerably more than my students did, I must speak of Buddhism. The cry often went up from students and faculty alike that if Exeter was to offer courses in religion, it should offer them also in comparative religion. Hinduism, Judaism, Islam—why shouldn't they all be studied side by side with Christianity so that students could make an intelligent choice among them? Not least of the many objections that sprang to my lips was that I didn't know enough about most other religions to choose intelligently among them myself, with the one exception of Buddhism. Through an earlier interest in Zen, which was very much in vogue then, I had gone on to some reading in the great Theravada and Mahayana schools, and over the course of my years at Exeter I did a good deal more reading still, the result of which was that I ended up feeling that, if I hadn't been a Christian, I would have been a Buddhist myself. And I feel that way still.

What made Buddhism such a valuable subject to study along with Christianity was that it was both so like it in some ways and so different in others that to study the two side by side was, both by comparison and by contrast, to discover something new about each. Christian ideas that students thought of as stale and obvious through having been overexposed to them since childhood took on new life when they, or ideas very close to them, appeared with exotic Pali or Sanskrit names and a whole new set of images, myths, and parables to illustrate them. There were the four *Brahma viharas,* for instance. First, *metta,* or loving-kindness, the love that exists between equals, like the love of friend for friend or sister for sister. Then *karuna,* or compassion, the love that reaches downward, like the love of the rich for the poor or the successful person for the person who has failed. Then *mudita,* the upward-reaching love that shares another's joy rather than his sorrow, like the love of someone who has nothing for someone who has everything, the love of the old woman in her walker for the young woman jogging up the hill. Each can be thought of as involving a higher stage of spiritual development than the preceding until you come finally to *upekkha,* which both subsumes and transcends the earlier three—*upekkha* as the detached, dispassionate love which no longer makes or even recognizes distinctions of any kind but loves all people impartially whether they are torturers of children or great humanitarians. There is something a little too cold-blooded and inscrutable about it to equate it with the Christian concept of *agape* as God's love that shines forth on both the just and the unjust or Christ's love even for his crucifiers, but the difference as well as the resemblance is illuminating and, for me, illuminated something of the kind of love I had observed in the East Harlem saints.

More moving, because it takes a form less intellectual than mythic, is the Mahayana concept of the *bodhisattva* as one who, after endless rebirths into the world of ignorance and suffering, finally unselfs himself to the point where he is ready to leave the wheel of rebirth forever and enter the ineffable bliss of Nirvana, but who chooses instead to postpone his escape indefinitely so that he can return again and again into the ever-recurring death and pain of things until the last blade of grass, even, has realized its buddha-nature and is ready for Nirvana as well, which is the destiny of all creatures in a universe that is, above all else, a buddha-making universe. "Though he was in the form of God, [he] emptied himself, taking the form of a servant . . . became obedient unto death, even death on a cross,"[12] says Saint Paul, who elsewhere, as a way of pointing out that it is above all else a Christ-making universe, says that the work of God will go on "until we all attain to mature manhood, to the measure of the stature of the fullness of Christ."[13] They are not the same thing by a long shot, but each helps to drive back a little the shadows in the other, and, by placing them alongside one another, you glimpse the deep holiness and truth, of which, as different attempts to speak what cannot ultimately be spoken, they are both only shadows themselves.

Finally, lest students of comparative religion be tempted to believe that to compare them is to discover that at their hearts all religions are finally one and that it thus makes little difference which one you choose, you have only to place side by side Buddha and Christ themselves.

Buddha sits enthroned beneath the Bo-tree in the lotus position. His lips are faintly parted in the smile of one who has passed beyond every power in earth or heaven to touch him. "He who loves fifty has fifty woes, he who loves ten has ten woes, he who loves none has no woes," he has said.[14] His eyes are closed.

Christ, on the other hand, stands in the garden of Gethsemane, angular, beleaguered. His face is lost in shadows so that you can't even see his lips, and before all the powers in earth or heaven he is powerless. "This is my commandment, that you love one another as I have loved you," he has said.[15] His eyes are also closed.

The difference seems to me this. The suffering that Buddha's eyes close out is the suffering of the world that Christ's eyes close in and hallow. It is an extraordinary difference, and even in a bare classroom in Exeter, New Hampshire, I think it was as apparent to everyone as it was to me that before you're done, you have to make a crucial and extraordinary choice.

In January of that first winter in Exeter, our first child was born. She was a girl, to be named Katherine after my mother, and to the last of my days I will remember that first of hers. I had been up all night. Sometime after dawn they told me I could come see her. I was shown down a long, empty corridor. A nurse held her up to the plate-glass window so that I could look at her from where I stood on the other side of it. Her face was puffy and flushed, her eyes swollen shut as though she had just come through some sort of punishing battle, which of course she had. I remember thinking that all my past and Judy's past and the past of all the people I had loved most in my life were caught up in her and that from that moment forward my life would never be the same again, as indeed it never has. She looked beat-up and exhausted. I think she was sleeping. With the glass between us, I could not touch her. She weighed less than my briefcase. She was the hope of the world. Tears leapt to my eyes as if I had been struck.

"He who loves fifty has fifty woes . . . who loves none has no woe," said the Buddha, and it is true. To love another, as you love a child, is to become vulnerable in a whole new way. It is no longer only through what happens to yourself that the world can hurt you but through what happens to the one you love also and greatly more hurtingly. When it comes to your own hurt, there are always things you can do. You can put up a brave front, for one, and behind that front, if you are lucky, if you persist, you can become a little brave inside yourself. You can become strong in the broken places, as Hemingway said.[16] You can become philosophical, recognizing how much of your troubles you have brought down on your own head and resolving to do better by yourself in the future. Like King Lear on the heath, you can become compassionate. Like the whiskey priest, you can become a saint. But when it comes to the hurt of a child you love, you are all but helpless. The child makes terrible mistakes, and there is very little you can do to ease his pain, especially when you are so often a part of his pain as the child is also part of yours. There is no way to make him strong with such strengths as you may have found through your own hurt, or wise through such wisdom, and even if there were, it would be the wrong way because it would be your way, not his. The child's pain becomes your pain, and as the innocent bystander, maybe it is even a worse pain for you, and in the long run even the bravest front is not much use.

What man and woman, if they gave serious thought to what having children inevitably involves, would ever have them? Yet what man and woman, once having had them and loved them, would ever want it otherwise? Because side by side with the Buddha's truth is the Gospel truth that "he who does not love remains in death."[17] If by some magic you could eliminate the pain you are caused by the pain of someone you love, I for one cannot imagine working such magic because the pain is so much a part of the love that the love would be vastly diminished, unrecognizable, without it. To suffer in love for another's suffering is to live life not only at its fullest but at its holiest. "One mustn't have human affections—or rather one must love every soul as if it were one's own child," the whiskey priest thinks to himself as he says good-bye for the last time to his own daughter in Greene's novel. "The passion to protect must extend itself over a world."[18] The small, beat-up face that I saw for the first time that January morning in 1959 actually was the face of the world if I'd only had a saint's eyes to see it with.

Eighteen months later another daughter was born, named Dinah, and four years later another still, named Sharman, and when John Poggio, the butcher, asked the sex of the third, he said, "Well, Reverend, I guess that's just the way the cookie crumbles," but, luckily for us all, that's not the way I felt. A man is supposed to want sons to carry on his name, but if at some level that was ever a concern of mine, I must have hoped that my books would carry on my name instead and never felt I needed to be consoled for having only daughters. The five of us were a family in a way that, as a child, my own family had never been, mainly because we lived in the same white clapboard house at 17 Main Street all those Exeter years instead of moving from place to place every year as my parents had done, and because instead of being away at work from nine to five like my father, who saw us only evenings and weekends, my work was only across the street, and I was in and out of home all day. It was a world apart from the world of classes and preaching and the endless debates over required church, and there is no need to say much about it because although every un-happy family is unhappy in its own way, as Tolstoy said, happy families are all alike, and there has been no time in my life when I was ever happier.

I knew that it couldn't last forever, but that made it seem only the more precious, and I can remember moments of our being all together when, even though I knew that the children would grow up someday and we would be scattered, I knew also that there was something about those moments that would never end. Like the moment of saying good-bye to my old friend on that New York street corner, which in some sense I have never left, there is a part of me that still crawls on all fours along the sandy beach at Little Boar's Head with two little girls on my back and a third asleep in Judy's lap. Summers we spent in Vermont, where we had a cottage in Rupert on a farm that her family owned there, and in an ancient World War II jeep we would go rattling through the woods and across the meadows to secret places which, even twenty years later, still ring with the sounds we made and which, in their silence, to this day, still keep some of our secrets. Christmas vacations, too, were in Vermont, and in those years, unlike more recent ones, one snow would fall on another with little thawing in between until eventually you could coast on sleds over the tops of the post and rail fences and, when the horses were let out of the stable, they would nicker and snort up to their chests in drifts and fill the air with blizzards when they cantered out into the white pasture. It is more than just memory, I think, that binds us to the past. The past is the place we view the present from as much as the other way around, and nothing I heard Tillich say about eternity was as eloquent as what was said by such times as those, where past, present, and future are all caught up together in a single timelessness.

From June of 1963 to September of 1964, we took a year off from Exeter, and again it was to Vermont that we went. For Judy as well as for me, the pace of school life was sometimes killing, and after four years it seemed time for a break. I also wanted to try my hand at another novel since I had had no time to do anything in that line since *Ansel Gibbs* some six years earlier. I was sitting on the living-room couch, trying to get on with it, when the phone rang, and it was a friend calling to ask if we had heard the news. The president had been shot, she said. He was in a hospital in Dallas. He was not expected to last out the day. No one who lived through that time can ever forget it, of course, or those few days that followed it when the world stood still, and everybody remembers just where they were and what they were doing when the news came through. I remember reading that when that old war-horse Andrei Gromyko signed the memorial volume at the American Embassy in Moscow, there were tears in his eyes, and I have no doubt they were real tears, just as the tears in Judy's eyes and mine were real too as we wandered around the house trying to hide them from the children and each other. When we ran into people we knew at the post office or the grocer's, even into strangers, it was like meeting at a family funeral.

But the novel I threw to the side when the phone rang I picked up soon again, as people everywhere picked up whatever they had thrown aside, and by the fall when it was time to go back to Exeter, I had finished it, entitling it *The Final Beast* from a poem of Stephen Crane's. As the first book I had done since entering the ministry, it was in some ways a departure from its three predecessors, and in explaining what I mean by that, I feel I must speak with unusual care. As I have long since discovered, the world is full of people—many of them, I regret to say, book reviewers—who, if they hear that a minister has written a novel, feel that they know, even without reading it, what sort of a novel it must be. It must be essentially a sermon with illustrations in the form of character and dialogue, and, as such, its view of life must be one-sided, simplistic, naive, with everything subordinated to the one central business of scoring some kind of homiletical bull's-eye. I protest that, in my case anyway, this simply is not so. Since my ordination, as well as before, novels, for me, start—as Robert Frost said his poems did—with a lump in the throat. I don't start with some theological axe to grind, but with a deep, wordless feeling for some aspect of my own experience that has moved me. Then, out of the shadows, a handful of characters starts to emerge, then various possible relationships between them, then a setting maybe, and lastly, out of those relationships, the semblance at least of a plot. Like any other serious novelist, I try to be as true as I can to life as I have known it. I write not as a propagandist but as an artist.

On the other hand—and here is where I feel I must be so careful—since my ordination I have written consciously as a Christian, as an evangelist, or apologist, even. That does not mean that I preach in my novels, which would make for neither good novels nor good preaching. On the contrary, I lean over backwards not to. I choose as my characters (or out of my dreams do they choose me?) men and women whose feet are as much of clay as mine are because they are the only people I can begin to understand. As a novelist no less than as a teacher, I try not to stack the deck unduly but always let doubt and darkness have their say along with faith and hope, not just because it is good apologetics—woe to him who tries to make it look simple and easy—but because to do it any other way would be to be less than true to the elements of doubt and darkness that exist in myself no less than in others. I am a Christian novelist in the same sense that somebody from Boston or Chicago is an American novelist. I must be as true to my experience as a Christian as black writers to their experience as blacks or women writers to their experience as women. It is no more complicated, no more sinister than that. As to *The Final Beast,* the part of the Christian experience that I particularly tried to make real was the one I found so conspicuously absent in most of the books I searched through for readings to assign my Exeter classes, and that was the experience of salvation as grace, as the now-and-thenness and here-and-thereness of the New Being.

Terrible things happen in the book—a Jewish woman is crippled by torture in a Nazi concentration camp, good people die cruel and pointless deaths. And wonderful things that might happen never quite do —a young minister who believes himself to be on the threshold of a religious vision ends up simply hearing the sound of two apple branches clacked together by the wind. But out of it all something no less precious for being as elusive and ambiguous as the clacking branches shines through a little here and there: a young woman who has believed herself sterile conceives a child, the young minister who has fled God, you feel, no less than his congregation because he is bored and fed-up returns with faith enough at least, he hopes, to get by on. "Whatever it is we move around through," he says to a friend. "Reality . . . the air we breathe . . . this emptiness . . . I think the dance that must go on back there, way down deep at the heart of space where being comes from. . . . If we saw any more of that dance than we do, it would kill us sure. The glory of it. Clack-clack is all a man can bear."[19]

The other part of my experience as a Christian that I tried to deal with in the novel was the experience of prayer, and, as in the episode of the apple branches, I drew directly from an event in my own life. A year or so before writing the book, I took two or three days off to attend a series of seminars on prayer conducted by an Episcopal laywoman named Agnes Sanford, who was recommended to me by a friend as a fascinating and deeply spiritual woman who had had remarkable success as a faith healer. "Spiritual" was another of those words that I always choked on a little, and faith-healing was something I associated with charlatans and the lunatic fringe; but since my friend had only recently left the college chaplaincy to become a Jungian analyst, I couldn't dismiss him as easily taken in, so I decided to accept his recommendation and go.

I saw Agnes Sanford first in the dingy front hall of the building where the talks were to take place, and after no more than a few minutes' conversation with her, I felt as sure as you can ever be in such matters that if there was such a thing as the Real Article in her line of work, then that was what she was. She was rather short and on the plump side with a breezy matter-of-factness about her which was the last thing I would have expected. She had far more the air of a college dean or a successful business-woman than of a Mary Baker Eddy or Madam Blavatsky. She seemed completely without pretensions, yet just as completely confident that she knew what she was talking about. She had an earthy sense of humor. She could be quite sharp when people asked her silly questions. Whether or not I would be able to believe in what she was to say about healing I had no way of knowing, but from the start there was no doubt that I believed in her.

The most vivid image she presented was of Jesus standing in church services all over Christendom with his hands tied behind his back and unable to do any mighty works there because the ministers who led the services either didn't expect him to do them or didn't dare ask him to do them for fear that he wouldn't or couldn't and that their own faith and the faith of their congregations would be threatened as the result. I recognized immediately my kinship with those ministers. A great deal of public prayer seemed to me a matter of giving God something that he neither needed nor, as far as I could imagine, much wanted. In private I prayed a good deal, but for the most part it was a very blurred, haphazard kind of business—much of it blubbering, as Dr. Muilenburg had said his was, speaking words out of my deepest needs, fears, longings, but never expecting much back by way of an answer, never believing very strongly that anyone was listening to me or even, at times, that there was anyone to listen at all.

That was the whole point, Agnes Sanford said. You had to expect. You had to believe. As in Jesus' parables of the Importunate Friend and the Unjust Judge, you had to keep at it. It took work. It took practice, was in that sense not unlike the Buddhist Eightfold Path. More than anything else, it took faith. It was faith that unbound the hands of Jesus so that through your prayers his power could flow and miracles could happen, healing could happen, because where faith was, healing always was too, she said, and there was no power on earth that could prevent it. Inside us all, she said, there was a voice of doubt and disbelief which sought to drown out our prayers even as we were praying them, but we were to pray down that voice for all we were worth because it was simply the product in us of old hurts, griefs, failures, of all that the world had done to try to destroy our faith. More even than our bodies, she said, it was these hurtful memories that needed healing. For God, all time is one, and we were to invite Jesus into our past as into a house that has been locked up for years—to open windows and doors for us so that light and life could enter at last, to sweep out the debris of decades, to drive back the shadows. The healing of memories was like the forgiveness of sins, she said. Prayer was like a game, a little ridiculous the way she described it, but we were to play it anyway —praying for the healing both of ourselves and others— because Jesus told us to and because most of the other games we played were more ridiculous still and not half so useful.

We were to believe in spite of not believing. That was what faith was all about, she told us. "Lord, I believe; help thou mine unbelief," said the father of the sick son,[20] and though it wasn't much, Jesus considered it enough. The boy was healed. Fairy-tale prayers, she called them. Why not? Jesus prayers. The language of the prayer didn't matter, and her own language couldn't have been plainer or her prayers more unliterary and down-to-earth. Only the faith mattered. All of this she spoke with nothing wild-eyed or dramatic about her, but clearly, wittily, less like a mystic than like the president of a rather impressive club. And you could also get too much praying, too much religion, she said, and when that happened, the thing to do was just to put it aside for a while as she did and do something else. She herself read murder mysteries, she said. Or just collapsed.

Some of what she said I put into *The Final Beast* through a character named Lillian Flagg, but more importantly, when I got back to Exeter, I tried to put it also into practice. Every morning before school began, I would bicycle up Tan Lane to the school church, and there in that shabby old building—all by myself with breakfast coffee still warm in my stomach and trying to empty my mind of the thousand things I would have to start doing when the bell rang for classes—I would kneel in one of the creaking, varnished pews and pray simply for the power to pray, which was a gift of the Holy Spirit promised to us all, Agnes Sanford told us, telling us to look up the twelfth chapter of First Corinthians in case we had happened to miss it in seminary. I had never given much thought to the Holy Spirit before, but through her I came to see that it was crucial to everything else, "the Lord and Giver of Life" as the Nicene Creed has it, the power of God to empower us, to bring faith, hope, love alive, which, without the Spirit, can be little more in us than good dreams, gestures.

Did they work, those early morning prayers with breakfast on my breath? How can you ever be sure? How can you know what you would have been, what you would have done, if you hadn't prayed? I have very little of the mystic about me. I am such a hopelessly verbal person that even as I pray, I hear myself praying and worry about the words. I find it all but impossible to rise above the paragraphs of my own blubbering, to leave enough room between the lines of my own beseeching for even the Holy Spirit to squeeze through. Nothing ever happened that I could either see or hear happening although, like the time when the apple branches clacked, I prayed for something sometimes that I could see or hear, if only a flicker of light among the high rafters, a whisper of what might or might not be just a gust of New Hampshire wind. Is there anything there, wherever we pray to, to see us or hear us? "A burning and frigid, transparent and limited universe . . . beyond which all is collapse and nothingness," Camus wrote. Maybe that is the truth. Who can say? I can say only that I kept on doing it week after week and to a lesser degree, more haphazardly, dimly, without a bicycle, have kept on doing it ever since. Maybe that in itself is the miracle.

And in some sense it was surely a miracle too that, as time went by there at Exeter, and in a way that would have made my flesh crawl with hideous embarrassment if I had foreseen it earlier in my life, I found myself praying for the healing of others with my hands on their heads as Agnes Sanford had taught us, explaining to us that we are flesh as well as spirit and that the touch of a hand has its own holiness. I prayed for a young woman unhappy in her marriage, a sick boy, a friend so confused and depressed with her life that she could hardly get out of bed in the morning. Imagination is so much a part of creation that there is no reason why it shouldn't be part of the creation of a miracle too, I thought, and I tried, as I prayed, Agnes Sanford's technique of imagining them bathed in what she spoke of as a healing light, tried to imagine Jesus himself standing there beside them with his hands on my hands on their heads. Never pray "if it be thy will," she said, because of course wholeness and healing are always his will, and "Rise up and walk" was all he would say when he healed, never adding any ifs to it as doorways to doubt. One way or another, those few

I prayed for all rose up and walked, not always with a spring in their step and their heads held high, God knows, but rose up, walked anyway. Was it the prayers, or would they have walked anyway, because time itself is no mean healer after all? I do not know. Maybe I do not even want to know. It is God's business, not ours, to know, as it is his business, not ours, to heal.

And once in morning assembly I asked the whole school to pray in such a way. All eight hundred boys were there and the usual scattering of faculty, many of them no more given to praying to anybody for anything than most of the boys were. Two men on the faculty were dying, both of them with cancer. I asked that great room full of people to pray for their healing, tried to explain to them how it was a game of believing and imagining, a matter of faith. And they did. As nearly as I could tell, there wasn't one of them there who was not at least surprised, if nothing else, into praying the prayer I asked, and the silence of close to a thousand people praying is deeper and richer than the silence even of the stars.

There was no miracle. The two men were not healed in any apparent way. And when the time came a few weeks or months later, they both of them died. There was only the deep silence, the deep asking, the memory that may still persist in a few of the ones who were there, as it still persists in me, of something that did happen there as well as of something that didn't. A voice only just not heard? A glimmer of light only just not seen? A failure of many things, in any case, but beyond all doubt not a failure at least of hope, of faith, of something like love. And I cannot overstress the degree to which it was actually a kind of miracle simply that I was praying such a prayer in that enormous room at all—I for whom praying in front of others had always seemed so unnatural and awkward that I cringed with embarrassment the first time, while we were still living in New York, that I said grace out loud over a meal with nobody there but Judy to hear me.

There were other things besides prayer that I found myself doing for the first time at Exeter, and chief among them, I suppose, was preaching. After Dean Wicks' final retirement, I became the school minister as well as the chairman of the religion department, and although I followed the tradition of getting visiting ministers to preach at the school church two or three Sundays out of each month—the most varied and effective ones I could find —at least one Sunday a month the job was mine, and I can still remember the sheer terror of it. They were so bright, those three hundred-odd boys, in some cases so much more so, I was afraid, than I was myself. And they were so literate. And, worse still, most if not all of them were there so much against both their wills and their principles, with somebody from the dean's office to check attendance and to wreak terrible vengeance on them if they were absent or late. There were also, in addition to the few faculty members who came regularly because they wanted to, others of them who came every once in a while because they felt they ought to or simply out of curiosity. They were often jaded, skeptical, sometimes even quite openly negative about the whole religious enterprise, but I was their friend and colleague, after all, and I suppose they thought there was always the off-chance that someday I might say something worth hearing. All in all, it was a sobering group to face on a Sunday morning.

Many of those early Exeter sermons were published later in a couple of volumes called *The Magnificent Defeat* and *The Hungering Dark,* so as far as the content of what I found to preach about is concerned, the record is available. But beyond what I actually said in those sermons, I have wondered sometimes about what was in the back of my head as I sat in the library in a deep leather armchair with my feet on the radiator trying to figure out how to say it. How did I approach my task? How did I think about the people I was saying it to? More than anything else, I think, I was influenced by a short piece of Karl Barth's called *The Need for Christian Preaching,* which I had read in seminary. "What are you doing, you man, with the word of *God* upon *your* lips?" Barth asks with italics and exclamation points flying. "Upon what grounds do you assume the role of mediator between heaven and earth? Who has authorized you to take your place there and to generate religious feeling? And, to crown all, to do so with results, with success? Did one ever hear of such overweening presumption, such Titanism, or—to speak less classically but more clearly—such brazenness! . . . One does not with impunity usurp the prerogative of God! . . . Can a minister be saved? I would answer that with men this is impossible [and although] with God all things are possible . . . so far as I know, there is no one who deserves the wrath of God more abundantly than the ministers."[21] It was a good place to start, I thought—the sheer arrogance and madness of the thing I was doing as I got to my feet and stepped into the pulpit in my new black robe from Bentley and Simon, religious outfitters, with the choir at my back, my heart in my mouth, and that great patchwork of faces in the pews in front of me.

It is precisely that moment that Barth so compellingly evokes. The minister steps into place. The congregation is silent. What have they come in search of? Barth asks. "Entertainment and instruction?" he proposes. "Very strange entertainment and instruction it is. Edification? So they say, but what is edification? Do they know? Do they really know at all why they are here?"[22] In the case of Exeter, many of them knew well enough, needless to say. They were there because the dean's office would get them if they weren't. But Barth's question still held for them, too, I thought, because did they really know why in the mind of the dean's office, of their parents, of the church at large, it seemed so important for them to be there? I think not. *Expectancy,* Barth says. That is why they were there, why all of us were. At that strange, still moment just before the show starts, it is above all else expectancy that throbs in the stillness like a pulse. All those people out there in the pews—some hostile, some searching, some both at once; some young and some old —"their being there points to the event that is expected or appears to be expected, or at least, if the place be dead and deserted, was once expected here," Barth says,[23] and the event they await so expectantly is the sermon itself in which, whether they recognize it or not, they all of them want to find the answer to one question beyond all other questions, which is the question, Is it true? *Is it true?*

"Is it true," Barth says, "this sense of a unity in diversity, of a stationary pole amid changing appearances, of a righteousness not somewhere beyond the stars but in the events which are our present life? . . . Is it true, this talk of a loving and good God, who is more than one of the friendly idols whose rise is so easy to account for, and whose dominion is so brief?[24]. . . Is it true that there is in all things a meaning, a goal, and a God?"[25]

These words of Barth's were extremely powerful words to me, seemed extremely honest and, as far as I could tell, extremely true; and in all my preaching at Exeter and ever since I have been guided by them. I have never assumed that the people I talk to are so certain it is true that the question is not still very much alive for them. Is anyone ever that certain? I assume always that they want to know if it is true as much as I do myself. I assume that even the most religiously disillusioned and negative among them want it to *be* true as much as the relatively devout do—want to be shown it, want it to be made somehow flesh before their eyes, want to be able to rejoice in it for themselves. And it is because, at some level of their being, their wanting is so great that you must be so careful what you give them, and because your wanting to give is so great, too.

If you are any good at all with words—if you are any good at all as an actor, with an actor's power to move people, to fascinate people, to move them sometimes even to tears—you have to be so careful not to make it just a performance, however powerful. You have to remember that it is not what you are saying that it is important for them to believe in, but only God. You have to remember how Jesus consigned to the depths of the sea those who cause any who believe in him to sin and how one sin you might easily cause them is to believe in yourself instead. I wrote my sermons at great length and with great care. I learned to write in shorter, simpler sentences than I had in my books because a listener loses track otherwise. Though I never dared step into the pulpit without everything, including the Lord's Prayer and the announcements, fully written out in front of me, I learned to be free enough of my manuscript to be able to read it without appearing to do so. I put on the best performance I could, in other words, and preached with all the eloquence I could muster, not only to them, of course, but also to myself because much of what preachers say they say always to themselves, to keep their own spirits up, to answer their own souls' questions—the sermon as whistling in the dark. There were times when I felt that something better and truer than my words was speaking through my words. There were times when I felt they were only words. There were times when the words seemed to fall dead from my lips and other times when I could see only too clearly how effective they were being. And maybe I entirely misjudged which time was which. I don't know. I know only that Barth is surely right when he says that no one risks the wrath of God more perilously than the minister in the pulpit, and yet at the same time I know that, as a minister, there are few places I would rather be. The excitement and challenge of it. The chance that something better than what you are can happen, that something more than you know can be spoken and heard.

It was at Exeter, too, that for the first time I conducted a communion service, presiding over the table laid with a fair white cloth by a couple of faculty wives, and with the Pepperidge Farm bread that Judy and I had sliced up into little cubes in the kitchen at home, and the trays full of Welch's grape juice served in glass thimbles so that everybody could be served separately and antiseptically without leaving their seats. The symbolism couldn't be worse, I thought and still think, and it seemed a wretched way to do it. There should be real wine, of course, to warm the heart and stir the blood. There should be a common cup, germs be damned. People should come up to the table. Together. But even so, to stand in for Christ as host at that strange feast always moved me. "Come unto me, all ye who labor and are heavy laden. . . ." That means everybody. No one, not one, is left out.

And at Exeter for the first time too I christened people, buried people, married people, and at the marriage of my brother, Jamie, in New York, I didn't need Dr. Freud to explain what was afoot when I slipped and said, "Let us play" instead of "Let us pray." It was play in the sense that I couldn't believe that I was properly and effectively doing whatever it was that a minister is supposed to do on these solemn occasions, or that my brother and his wife would be properly married. It was play in the sense, too, of make-believe, and there, I think, my subconscious spoke with a wisdom of its own. To marry, bury, baptize people in the name of God is a kind of make-believe indeed. It is to play at believing that God is actually present at those most nakedly and movingly human moments to hallow them. It is to play out that outlandish notion not until you somehow manage to convince yourself that it is true, but until you begin to see that at the heart of your play there is truth the way there is truth at the heart of any play you put your heart into: truth about the heart itself, and about what the heart hungers for, and about what there is in the play that both whets and feeds the heart's hunger.

For a while the dean's office made an exception to the rule about required church. The edict was handed down that a student might attend a religious discussion group instead, and those groups were scheduled to take place before church in order to prevent boys from attending only so they could get a little more sleep on Sunday mornings. For that reason only the most radical dissenters attended, and it was one of those—a lean, freckle-faced senior—who turned to me once, thin-lipped with anger, and said, "So what's so good about religion anyway?" and I found myself speechless. I felt surely there must be something good about it. Why else was I there? But for the moment I couldn't for the life of me think what it was. Maybe the truth of it is that religion the way he meant it—a system of belief, a technique of worship, an institution—doesn't really have all that much about it that is good when you come right down to it, and perhaps my speechlessness in a way acknowledged as much.

Unless you become like a child, Jesus said, you will never enter the Kingdom of Heaven, and maybe part of what that means is that in the long run what is good about religion is playing the way a child plays at being grown up until he finds that being grown up is just another way of playing and thereby starts to grow up himself. Maybe what is good about religion is playing that the Kingdom will come, until—in the joy of your playing, the hope and rhythm and comradeship and poignance and mystery of it you start to see that the playing is itself the first-fruits of the Kingdom's coming and of God's presence within us and among us.

III

Vermont

AT THE END of nine years we decided to leave Exeter, and as the time approached, I found that night after night I was systematically dreaming my way through my friends on the faculty. When I mentioned this to the wife of one of them, she said that what I was doing was saying good-bye to them, and of course she was right. They had entered the part of me where my dreams come from, and although a number of years have gone by since then, some of them come ambling through my dreams still. Many deep ties had to be broken, that is to say, and, in the way of deep ties, many simply went underground. Our three daughters had been born there. We had put down roots. There was much in us that didn't want to say good-bye at all. But in the spring of 1967, we left. Why?

From one place to another place, from one task to another task, from one set of friends, of pleasures, of worries, to the next—maybe it is because of habits established by my peripatetic childhood that life has always seemed to be a matter of moving on. I suppose that was part of it. Another part of it was that with the day of negoism pretty much replaced by the student activism of the sixties, a lot of the tension had gone out of religion teaching and with it at least some of the excitement. The religion department was well established with an enrollment and faculty comparable to the art and music departments anyway, and that was a far cry from the handful of boys and one part-time teacher that it had been nine years earlier. I seem to remember figuring out that over the period of every three years or so, over half the student body would have taken one of our courses or another. Furthermore, I had been there long enough and did what I did acceptably enough so that everybody seemed more or less satisfied, and there was therefore no particular challenge from outside myself to do it any better or any differently. In sum, it was all, comparatively speaking, quite comfortable, and with those remnants of Puritan conscience that are part of us all, I decided that for that very reason it was probably time to move on to something else. It also seemed healthy for the school to have a new voice speaking to it of holy matters, a fresh approach, a different style.

The decision that had to be made, of course, was what I was going to leave it for, and what I decided was to try to do some writing again. There was no question for either Judy or me about Vermont being the place we wanted to live, and we both loved the idea of being there all year round for a while, watching the seasons change and not having to pack up and leave every September. But I had considerable misgivings about it, too. I was giving up a good job and burning my bridges behind me. I had a novel I wanted to write, but there is never any assurance that the words will flow when you want them to. And even if they did, was the writing of novels a fitting occupation for a minister anyway? Was I just leaving the comfortableness of Exeter for a life more comfortable still? Would I be writing for the glory of God or just for my own glory? To look at it another way, I would be on my own with no institution, no colleagues, to draw support from, with no bells ringing to remind me of my responsibilities, no structure to my life other than whatever structure I found it possible to impose on it myself. But we had decided to go, and go we did, and part of the power that impelled us was the power of Vermont itself, which we both of us loved, I since our marriage and Judy since she had started spending summers there with her family as a child.

Our house is on the eastern slope of Rupert Mountain, just off a country road, still unpaved then, and five miles from the nearest town. We look out across a horse pasture below the front lawn and a cow pasture that rises up to the shoulder of Oak Hill across the road from us. Beyond Oak Hill is another higher hill with a spine running down the side that faces us, which makes it look like the neck and shoulders of some great beast browsing its shaggy way toward us with its head hidden in the valley. Beyond that there is a low range of mountains— Dorset, Mother Myrick, Green Peak—alive with the shadows of clouds, the changing of light, the passing of seasons. Up in the hills behind us are acres of forest and meadowland crisscrossed here and there with tumbled stone walls left over from the days when people lived there and farmed it before the opening of the West lured them off to other acres richer and flatter and more farmable. The trees are mainly spruce and white birch and sugar maples that turn scarlet and russet in the fall. There is one high hill whose entire summit is covered with raspberries, and a soft green ridge, covered with blueberries, that looks west toward the far Adirondacks. There is a pond whose banks are purple with gentians in summertime, and a tunnel of spruce that in wintertime, when snow weighs the branches to the ground, becomes the Land of Narnia as the children first stepped into it through the magic wardrobe. There are miles of narrow jeep roads that years ago my father-in-law put in and named for old friends and neighbors—Marquand Road, Kouwenhoven Road, McCormick Road, Hatch Road, and even a Buechner Road, though named not for me but for an uncle of mine. Even at the most unpromising times of year—in mudtime, on bleak, snowless winter days—it is in so many unexpected ways beautiful that even after all this time I have never quite gotten used to it. I have seen other places equally beautiful in my time, but never, anywhere, have I seen one more so.

I fill this account with comings and goings, with people and ideas, with books I read and others I wrote, but for a long time now the background of my life has been these trees, meadows, and pastures, all the continual changings of which are only another form of their permanence, and which have nothing to do with ideas or books, and which suffer people to move among them, to be sure, but are in the long run as untouched by them as the sky is untouched by clouds. My wife knows them all by name. She knows the birds by their songs and can tell red pine from white pine without even trying. With her farm animals to look after, her vegetable garden and flowers to tend, she makes the place so much her life that to move to some other place would be to change her life profoundly. I, on the other hand, could do what I do anywhere. I could do it as easily in a New York apartment or a houseboat on the Nile. I try to learn the names of the wildflowers every spring and by the next spring find that I've forgotten them again. I love the view, but I'm never sure which mountain is which. I can get lost in the same woods I've been riding, skiing, walking through since 1956 because I have never really stopped to figure them out any more than as far as I can tell they have ever stopped to figure me out. And yet, in the back of my head, I know always that the place is there as more than just background because it has become a part of me as I have become part of it.

I go about my business, and it goes about its business, but though we are in countless ways removed from each other, we are by no means uninvolved with each other. When the leaves start to change in September, something in me starts to change with them. When some sorrow rises in my throat or some gladness makes my heart beat faster, the very indifference of the landscape becomes a kind of bond between us because it is *I* who am the one it is indifferent to, and my sorrows and gladnesses are reduced to size by its endless capacity for ignoring them. *So there is Buechner being himself* say the hills and fields, the horses and birds, the rain, the snow, the sun. *And there you are being yourselves too,* I say back. Such vast and unconditional acceptance of each other is not the same thing as love, I realize, any more than *upekha* is the same thing as *agape,* but it is not altogether unrelated either. In deep and mysterious ways, I think, neither of us would be quite the same without the other.

When we first started living there all year round in 1967, I was reluctant to believe that it would be our last move and that our house would be the one I would die in, but I have long since concluded that this will probably be the case and accept it with comparative equanimity. And I long ago concluded something else, too. The first few years we were there, the children were still little, and our problems with them, like theirs with us, seemed little too. They were healthy and happy, and so were we. Like everybody else they had their troubles at school, but basically they liked it well enough. They had their friends, and we had our friends, but the richest part of our lives seemed to be the part we had together—the picnics by the gentian pond, the sledding in winter, the summer trips. We were a world very much to ourselves up there on our mountain, and by and large all was well with us. But down below there was another world where, by and large, all was not well. Friends got sick and died there. Accidents happened to people we knew. Children not much older than ours got into all sorts of grief. Couples got divorced, and men lost their jobs. And farther away still, Vietnam happened, assassinations happened, Watergate happened, until there were times when it seemed to me as though the world below was a stormy sea with waves all around us as high as the hills we were encircled by, and the little patch of mountain where we lived was the only place left anywhere that was safe and dry. What I concluded then—less in a way to mar our peace than to deepen my sense of it—was that the day would come when the wild waves would wet us too, and the winds would lash us, and the great beast browsing its way up from below would raise its head and notice us at last. I concluded that even in Paradise, maybe especially in Paradise, the dark times come.

For me that first Vermont year was dark. A number of

people assumed that when I left Exeter, I was also leaving the ministry, and what unsettled me about that was, on the one hand, that it was not true—I had every hope of being as much a minister in the books I wrote as in the sermons I preached and the classes I taught—and, on the other hand, that I would have to work very hard and carefully to make sure that it did not become true. I couldn't just take my time and feel my way into the novel I had in mind. I had to write it as soon as I could, and it had to be not just another novel about this or that, but a novel in which I somehow gave life and power to the same vision of things that had led me to become a minister in the first place. So day after day, in a quiet room in the wing of our house, I sat down to my work half paralyzed by my sense of its crucial importance to me if no one else. I was not just a man writing a book, but a man watching a man writing a book and at the same time continually asking himself whether it was a book worth writing. To make matters still worse, that was the year when both Martin Luther King and Robert Kennedy were murdered, and I remember wondering if there was anything the world needed much less to have added to its pain than another book. At the same time, I started having the kind of neurotic fears about my health that writers in general seem prone to, I suppose because their eyes are so perpetually turned in upon themselves and their imaginations so overworked. I was sure I must be dying of some nameless disease, and even the reassurance of doctors was of little use. If I had nothing to worry about, then I would worry about not worrying. And I was lonely too, all of it. I missed having students and colleagues to bounce my life off of. At suppertime I had no tales to tell my wife and children about what had happened to me that day. My only adventures were the ones that took place inside my head.

Out of it all, by Caeserian section, I somehow managed to bring a novel forth anyway. *The Entrance to Porlock* I called it in reference to the visitor from Porlock who woke Coleridge out of the visionary trance of *Kubla Khan,* and what it was essentially about, I think, was the tension between everyday reality and the reality of dreams, of imagination. The plot was based loosely on *The Wizard of Oz.* An old man who runs a secondhand bookstore on a mountain like ours in Vermont sees the ghosts of dead writers whose books he sells, sees glimpses of a shimmering reality within reality, and in the process, loses touch with his family. He is the Tin Woodsman in search of a heart. One son, a pathetic failure and compulsive joker, is the Scarecrow in search of a brain. Another son, the bullying and hypochondriacal dean of a school like Exeter who fantasizes continually about receiving the farewell visits of friends as he lies dying in a hospital, is the Cowardly Lion in search of courage. And there is a grandson— confused, introverted, adolescent —who, like Dorothy, is in search of home, if only a home inside himself. The Wizard is an Austrian who runs a community for the mentally and emotionally disturbed, and it is in their relationship to him that they all move at least a step closer to finding what is missing in themselves.

Like all novels, I suppose, and like all dreams, it is symbolic autobiography, a strange, dense, slow-paced book, the labor of writing which was so painful that I find it hard, even now, to see beyond my memory of the pain to whatever merit it may have. But I remember still the feeling that in it I had written myself into a blank wall.

There was no farther I could go in that direction. And I felt that in a sense I had lived myself into a blank wall too. I was a minister without a church, a teacher without students, a writer without a subject. I looked to my wife and daughters for more than any human being can give to another. I felt like a rat in a trap, and the trap I was in was myself and the new life I had chosen.

How desperate, becalmed, cheerless that all sounds, and so it often seemed at the time. But what you tend to forget, looking back this way at key moments of your life, are all the other moments that appeared to be so unimportant by comparison and yet were in their own way no less keys themselves—were, in fact, the major part of your life. It was not just in the room where I struggled through *Porlock,* loneliness, hypochondria, that my life went on, and I have great quantities of evidence to prove it. I have miles of home movies and hundreds of photographs pasted in albums. I have diaries and letters. I have not just my own memory but the memories of my family and friends. Life went on all over the place, and woven in and out of the dark days were many of the brightest days I have ever known. There were birthdays—summer birthdays especially by the pool of my mother-in-law, known to her grandchildren as May, down the hill from our house with the children careening around, still too little for bathing suits, and balloons to blow up, and poppers to pop, and shameful numbers of presents to open. There were cosmic croquet games after Sunday lunch down there too, and the *Times* crossword to work in the hot Vermont sun. There were slapstick, noisy tennis games with our friends the Doles and expeditions with my friend John Kouwenhoven to secondhand bookstores off toward New Hampshire where we would spend hours at a stretch so lost in the dimness and dust of our browsing that if anybody had asked us our names, we would have had to stop to remember. And there were Christmases with the tree to chop down and lug back lashed to a toboggan, and an evil-tasting wassail which my brother, Jamie, and I insisted on making from a recipe of Charles Dickens and drank with our wives and mother while the three little girls strung popcorn on thread and made bangles out of golden Breck Shampoo cartons and hung up gingerbread replicas of their various animals—Katherine's goat, Millie, and Sharmy's favorite araucana hen, Ethel, and Dinah's pig, known as Piggy or Miss Piggy years before there was any other by that name and who was no bigger than our dachshund when we first brought her home in a sack but soon outweighed our refrigerator.

Friends from Exeter came to see us, and old friends from school and college days. Every summer we would visit our Hatch relatives in Maine where the horizontalness of sea and sand can ease the spirit in ways that not even the mountains have ever quite mastered; and every winter we'd spend a week or two at May's in Florida where you go to sleep with the slap and hiss of the waves in your ears and wake to the papery rattle of the wind in the palms. Happy the man whose mother-in-law turns out to be, not the comic-strip adversary, but as dear and valued a friend as any he has. And in the spring of 1968, while I was in the grim throes of *Porlock,* we took the children and my mother on a trip to Bermuda, where I had lived as a child some thirty years earlier. There, still, was the smoked salmon-colored house where we'd lived across the harbor from Hamilton, and Warwick Academy, where Jamie and I had gone to school, flying kites on the playing fields on Good Friday as the custom was, and learning how to spin wooden tops by winding the string tight and throwing them hard, and how to remember the major victories of the Duke of Marlborough by the mnemonic word BROM—Blenheim, Ramillies, Oudenarde, and Malplaquet. I have never forgotten them and never shall. It was no longer the enchanted island I had known as a child, Prospero's island. The cedars had gone with the blight. The little narrow-gauge railway had gone. With the coming of cars, trucks, motorcycles, where before there had been only bicycles and horse-drawn carriages and lorries, most of the marvelous smells had gone too and, with them, much of what had made the place greener and more dreamlike than any other place I have known since or ever hope to know. But still it was good to see it again, to catch stray glimpses of how it had been in the old days and to show it to my family. It gave back a fragment of the past.

When it came to my work, my ministry, writing books was not the only form it took. I continued to preach from time to time—at fancy places like Yale and Princeton and unfancy places like the small Congregational church in Rupert, where the thirty or so people who came of a Sunday and the creaking old organ and the swept and dusted shabbiness gave me often a richer sense of a place where God had been truly spoken to and heard than many a more Gothic and grander. I taught Sunday school in the deserted bar of an inn in Dorset and helped with religion conferences elsewhere. When some of the local churches were without a minister for one reason or another, I took weddings and funerals and christenings.

Every once in a while, people with problems who had never found their way to a church found their way to me precisely because I had no church and for that reason seemed to them more approachable. And I kept on trying to pray the way Agnes Sanford had taught me because I was helpless to do otherwise. So both at work and at play, life went on in many places other than the room where I wrote, in other words; there were memorable moments and unmemorable moments, and as far as my sense of being trapped is concerned, it was the unmemorable ones, the apparently random and everyday ones, that turned out to be the key moments, the key that let me out of the trap at last.

At about the time I was finishing *Porlock,* for the second time in my life I received a letter which, like the one from Dean Wicks when I was finishing at Union Seminary, changed the direction of my life. It was from a man named Charles Price, who was then the chaplain at Harvard, and his purpose was to invite me to give something called the Noble Lectures there the winter of 1969. If Harvard had invited me to come pick up gum wrappers with a pointed stick, I suppose I would have been flattered, and though I'd never heard of the Noble Lectures, the men who had given them in earlier years were a group to conjure with—Teddy Roosevelt, for some reason that was never made clear to me, had been the first, but from then on they had been people like H. Richard Niebuhr and George Buttrick, and even Paul Tillich had accepted the assignment but died before the time came round. Since I was hardly a theologian myself, let alone in anything remotely resembling the league of the others as I wrote Price, what could I possibly lecture about if I decided to risk lecturing at all? Perhaps something in the area of "religion and letters," he wrote back, and it was the word *letters* that did it.

What he meant by the word was clear enough, but suddenly I found myself thinking of letters literally instead— of letters as the alphabet itself, the A's, B's, C's, and D's out of which all literature, all words, are ultimately composed. And from there I wandered somehow to the notion of the events of our lives— even, and perhaps especially, the most everyday events—as the alphabet through which God, of his grace, spells out his words, his meaning, to us. So *The Alphabet of Grace* was the title I hit upon, and what I set out to do was to try to describe a single representative day of my life in a way to suggest what there was of God to hear in it. I accepted the invitation, in any case, and what I stood up at that exalted lectern in Memorial Church to lecture about was simply what it was like to be me: to get up in the morning— washing, dressing, waking the children; to go off to my mongrel labors as minister-writer; to think my thoughts and dream my dreams and worry my worries; and finally to come home again. Evening and morning, one day. My day. There were to be three lectures, and I named them *gutturals, sibilants,* and, thinking of the Hebrew alphabet, *the absence of vowels* to suggest something about the harshness, the subtlety, and the mystery of the events through which God speaks to us all. It was, of course, a preposterous subject, as I look back on it, but for some reason I didn't allow myself to think of that at the time and simply went ahead and did it with results that, at least for me, were of considerable significance.

By examining as closely and candidly as I could the life that had come to seem to me in many ways a kind of trap or dead-end street, I discovered that it really wasn't that at all. I discovered that if you really keep your eye peeled to it and your ears open, if you really pay attention to it, even such a limited and limiting life as the one I was living on Rupert Mountain opened up onto extraordinary vistas. Taking your children to school and kissing your wife good-bye. Eating lunch with a friend. Trying to do a decent day's work. Hearing the rain patter against the window. There is no event so commonplace but that God is present within it, always hiddenly, always leaving you room to recognize him or not to recognize him, but all the more fascinatingly because of that, all the more compellingly and hauntingly. In writing those lectures and the book they later turned into, it came to seem to me that if I were called upon to state in a few words the essence of everything I was trying to say both as a novelist and as a preacher, it would be something like this: Listen to your life. See it for the fathomless mystery that it is. In the boredom and pain of it no less than in the excitement and gladness: touch, taste, smell your way to the holy and hidden heart of it because in the last analysis all moments are key moments, and life itself is grace. What I started trying to do as a writer and as a preacher was more and more to draw on my own experience not just as a source of plot, character, illustration, but as a source of truth.

Depression, desperation, anxiety. The sense of my life as flat and irrelevant. Doubts about myself and doubts about my work. It is by no means true that those Harvard lectures drove the shadows away once and for all. This side of Nirvana, there is no such escape for any of us as far as I know. But the shadows themselves contain treasures if you keep your eyes open, and in addition to the lectures themselves, one treasure I found among them and that saw me through many a shadowy time yet to come was both a new place to work and, along with it, a new place within myself, a new power for working. Our youngest daughter, Sharman—named for a fierce old forty-niner who was her great-greatgrandfather—started attending that year a morning class for preschool children at the Episcopal church in Manchester some fifteen miles away from where we lived. Instead of leaving her there at nine or whatever and coming back to get her at noon, I asked Robert Clayton, the rector, if it might be possible for me to stay and do my work there. On the second floor of the parish house there was a library, he said, and I was welcome to use it. I accepted his offer and spent the next ten years or so of my working life up there.

The library turned out to be a rather small room with not much in it except for the bookshelves, a scarred blackboard, a table, and some uncomfortable folding chairs mixed in with some pint-sized kindergarten chairs, but places are as full of mystery as times are, and almost from the start I knew that, of all places, it was the one that was right for me. The parish house seemed more part of the real working world than home ever had and thus made it easier to believe that maybe my work was real too. It was a place to put on a necktie for and to come home from. I could hear Bob Clayton and his wife, Betty, at work in the office downstairs, and the sounds of the typewriter, the telephone, and the comings and goings of the parish helped me believe in my more sanguine moments that, obscure and crackpot as my labors were, they might still have some remote, second-story connection at least with the church of Christ. And more perhaps than anything else, there were morning prayers.

Except on the rarest occasions, nobody ever came to them but Bob and me. The first thing every morning we would trudge across the grass to the church and ring the bell. On some days he would read the service and I the responses. On others we would reverse the procedure. *The Lord be with you. And with thy spirit. O come let us sing. Let us pray.* The psalms. The readings from the lectionary. The silences. At first I had the idea that my primary purpose in driving those fifteen miles every morning was to write and that the prayers were incidental, but later on I came to suspect that maybe the other way 'round was closer to the truth. And later on still, I was less sure than I had been that in the long run there was all that much difference between the writing and the praying anyway. In any case, most of what I wrote for the next ten years I wrote in that small, bare room, after those small, bare services, and on the few occasions when I have looked in on the room since, I've realized that part of me will always be homesick for it.

And part of me will always be homesick, too, for a person I came to know, also in Manchester, during those same years. When the Baptist church, of which she was a member, was without a minister one winter, I took the services every Sunday for a few months, and that was how we met. She was a woman well on into her seventies, very thin, very stooped. She had been married a number of times, and for years, as a widow, had been living alone, on welfare, in the one small apartment left inhabitable in a house that had been gutted by fire a few years earlier. Shaking hands at the church door after the service one

Sunday morning, I had said to her—neither expecting nor much caring about an answer—"How are you?" and she looked up at me out of her wry, beleaguered old face and said, "As well as can be expected." Just that and no more, then made her way down the steps and out into the cold.

I am as deaf as the next one and usually deafer when it comes to calls for help, but I was all she had by way of a minister just then, after all, and I was not so literary and detached and specialized as not to know that every once in a while, if only to keep their hands in, Christians are supposed to be Christs to each other for Christ's sweet sake, so I steeled myself and went to call on her one winter afternoon. I expected the worst, of course, because that is my nature. I expected a long, dreary monologue. I expected plenty of complaints with some tears to go with them. I expected to feel awkward and inadequate. I expected to be bored and hoped to get away as soon as I decently could. And I couldn't possibly have been more wrong on every count. None of the things I expected to happen happened, and none of the things I expected to feel did I feel, neither on that first day I went to see her nor on all the other days I went to see her from that time on until finally, around Saint Valentine's day some seven or eight years later, she died, and I conducted her burial service before a little knot of family and friends under a gray Vermont sky with the wind flapping my black robe around my ankles.

She had worked as a cook for a while when she was younger and stronger, and she told me one day how some guest of the lady she worked for complimented her once on a dish she had made by telling her that it was really very nice in its way, but that it was also, of course, really very crude. "Very *crude!* Very *crude!*" my old friend parodied her all those years later, croaking like a parrot at the outrage and absurdity and truth of what she remembered. "Of course it was crude!" she said. "Everything I do is crude. I am crude," and in some sublime sense I suppose she was right. Her chest rattled from congestive heart failure when she breathed, and when she had to spit up into a wad of the toilet paper roll she kept by her chair because it was cheaper than Kleenex, she spat up. If there were things on her mind that she had to spit up, she spat them up too. She spoke from her heart. She called a spade a spade. She told the truth. She was crude the way the riches of the earth are crude before they have been refined into something less rich by far. She was also courteous the way a great queen is courteous because she knew no other way to be—courteous in the sense that she listened with her heart when you talked, never burdening you with her own burdens but ready to hear you out to the end if ever you felt like unburdening yourself to her. *Aggravation* was the title of the game we always played on a homemade wooden board she had with unmatching dice which we shook in a pair of the little plastic jars her heart pills came in, but it was the only form of aggravation she allowed herself to dwell upon although she had known plenty of it in her time and had had more than her share of sorrow and loss. But she rarely talked of the past unless I pressed her to and never once that I remember talked of it with either bitterness or self-pity. Her usual subjects were just whatever came up —the weather, the people who had dropped in that day, what had happened at church or the senior citizens when she was still able to walk that far.

Every time I came we prayed the Lord's Prayer together at the end of my visit, sitting there knee to knee in our two chairs and holding hands because that was the way she and her last and favorite husband had done it, she said, and because it helped her concentrate. Then at some point before I left, she always made the same remark. "Oh, you don't know how much good it does me to have you come!" she would cry out, then bury her head in her lap, her face in her hands, and shake with whatever it was that shook her at such times. But she was as unsentimental as anybody I've ever known and in seconds had bobbed up again and was off to the next thing—a jar of dandelion greens she wanted me to take home with me, maybe, or a piece by Oral Roberts she thought I might like. What good it did her to have me come, as she said, I have no way of knowing, but I cannot believe it surpassed the good she did me. To this day I can't pass her old house on Bonnet Street—all fixed up now and trim with a coat of new paint—without wanting to cover my face with my hands and shake like a tree in the wind.

Listen to your life.

All moments are key moments.

You sit down at your desk in front of your typewriter, or if, like me, you don't use a desk and a typewriter, you sit down wherever you sit down with a pad of paper in your lap and a pen in your hand. Is it a book you are going to write, or a letter to a friend, or a diary, if you keep one? Or are you sitting down not to write anything at all, maybe, but just to think, to remember, or just to pray, maybe, which is another kind of thinking, another way of remembering? Whichever it is you sit down to, the process is much the same. Writing, thinking, remembering, praying—you need words for all of them. Words are put together out of letters, all twenty-six of them. So the alphabet is your instrument. Everything you have it in you to say must be said by means of A's and B's and C's and D's. By means of vowels and consonants, you must put together the best words you can—words that, if possible, not only mean something but evoke something, call something forth from the person you address with your words. Christ himself both spoke such a word and was such a word.

Words—especially religious words, words that have to do with the depth of things—get tired and stale the way people do. Find new words or put old words together in combinations that make them heard as new, make you yourself new, and make you understand in new ways. "Blessed are the meek" are the words of the English translators—words of great beauty and power—but over the years they have become almost too familiar to hear any more. *"Heureux sont les debonnaires"* are the French words—Blessed are the debonair—and suddenly new beauty, new power, flood in like light. Blessed is Fred Astaire in white tie and tails. Blessed is Oliver Hardy in rusty black suit and derby hat as he picks his dapper way toward the unseen banana peel on the sidewalk. Blessed is my old friend as she tries to let me win at Aggravation, rattling her dice in the cup which the pills that keep her alive come in. Arrange the alphabet into words that are true in the sense that they are true to what you experience to be true. If you have to choose between words that mean more than what you have experienced and words that mean less, choose the ones that mean less because that way you leave room for your hearers to move around in and for yourself to move around in too.

There is also the alphabet of your life—the gutturals that jar, hurt, deaden; the sibilants that gladden, raise up, enchant; the vowelessness that may be only the east wind rattling the branches or may be the stirring of miracle. What are the words, what is the meaning, that this living alphabet of events spells out?—not meaning in the sense of a lesson to be drawn, a moral to be appended, but meaning in the sense of what your life means to you, of what your life is telling you about yourself? The puzzling out of such hieroglyphics and the translating of them into ABC—whether written or spoken, books or prayers—is not easy and not something you should spend so much time at that listening to your life gets in the way of living your life. I have spent an enormous amount of time at it since we first moved to Vermont, and who can say what I have both gained by it and lost by it, or how I could have spent my time more profitably? The might-have-been of things is blessedly not ours to know. But for going on fifteen years now, I have sat for five or six hours each working day with my pen in my hand. And sometimes I have been lucky.

I was lucky with *The Alphabet of Grace* because, with his phrase about religion and *letters,* Charles Price gave me more by way of a subject than he can have realized, and compared with the wretched time I'd had with *Porlock,* those lectures all but wrote themselves. Some years later I was asked to give a similar set of lectures at Yale. Preaching was what they were supposed to be about, and though I found that subject harder than the other because it wasn't just the randomness of my life that I had to listen to now, but my life specifically with the Gospel and my struggles to understand and speak about it, that book also was an answer to somebody else's question and, for that reason, easier to handle than the kind of question you ask yourself or that your life asks you. *Telling the Truth* I called it, and in it I tried to speak of how, with its message that, without God, all mankind labors and is heavy laden, the Gospel must be heard as tragedy first before it can be heard as a comedy in which all are given rest if they will only come unto him, and as a fairy tale last of all in which, as I put it, impossible things happen to impossible people, the beautiful queen is exposed in all her wickedness at last and the ugly duckling is transformed into a swan.

A great deal of my teaching at Exeter had involved no more than simply trying to clarify the meaning of some of the great religious words because somewhere along the line—sometimes, I'm afraid, not just out of the air but out of Sunday School and sermons—many of the boys I taught had picked up what struck me as such distortions of those words that they seemed entirely justified in rejecting them. Sin was not basically sex, I tried to explain to them, any more than faith was the capacity to swallow certain holy whoppers that an intelligent eighth grader would dismiss out of hand, so some years afterwards, out of my memory of those classes, I put together a kind of theological ABC, which I called *Wishful Thinking* and in which I tried again to define some of those great words not in any definitive or heavily theological way but in as fresh a way as I could find for restoring to them some of their original life and depth and power. Later on, in a book called *Peculiar Treasures,* and drawing again on my teaching days, I tried to do the same thing with a hundred or so characters out of the Bible, beginning with Aaron and ending with Zaccheus—tried to scrape off some of the veneer with which centuries of reverence had encrusted them until I reached something at least approaching, I hoped, what had once been their flesh-and-blood humanity. Our daughter Katherine did a pen-and-ink illustration for each, which in some cases struck me as more telling than my words. It is by no means true that these books were all that easy to write—I had to work, perhaps too hard, at being brief, gnomic, lively—but much of what I had to do was simply to reach back to what I remembered from my Exeter years and to questions I had tried to answer then and to my own questioning.

And something like that same process was involved in the case of one other book that I did at about this same time when I was approached by a publisher to supply a text to accompany a beautifully reproduced set of color photographs of various attempts over the centuries to depict the likeness of Christ. *The Faces of Jesus* was what it was to be called, and the collection of pictures it contained was rich and varied—primitive African carvings, Renaissance paintings, medieval tapestries and vestments, a scrimshaw crucifixion, a head of Jesus painted on the slatted overhead door of a garage—some of them deeply moving, some of them tasteless and terrible, some of them fascinatingly both. They were sent to me divided into groups—the nativity, the ministry, the Last Supper, and so on—and what I found myself doing by way of a text was writing not in any sense either a scholar's life of Christ or a complete life, but as much of a life as emerged from the pictures themselves. And that is much of what, for me, the writing process more or less always involves.

There is the craft of it, to be sure—the labor of arranging the twenty-six letters into the most accurate, most alive words I can find—but prior to that there is the much less conscious and effortful business of simply looking out at the alphabet of my own experience and responding to it, as in *The Faces of Jesus* I responded to the pictures and as in *Wishful Thinking* and *Peculiar Treasures* I responded to my memories of teaching at Exeter. And it is with this prior part of the process especially that luck comes in, if luck is what you want to call it, because it is looking out at, looking down into, that you never know what may float to the surface next.

I was reading a magazine as I waited my turn at a barber shop one day when, triggered by a particular article and the photographs that went with it, there floated up out of some hitherto unexplored subcellar of me a character who was to dominate my life as a writer for the next six years and more. He was a plump, bald, ebullient southerner who had once served five years in a prison on a charge of exposing himself before a group of children and was now the head of a religious diploma mill in Florida and of a seedy, flat-roofed stucco church called the Church of Holy Love, Incorporated. He wore a hat that looked too small for him. He had a trick eyelid that every once in a while fluttered shut on him. His name was Leo Bebb.

I had never known a man like Leo Bebb and was in most ways quite unlike him myself, but despite that, there was very little I had to do by way of consciously, purposefully inventing him. He came, unexpected and unbidden, from a part of myself no less mysterious and inaccessible than the part where dreams come from; and little by little there came with him a whole world of people and places that was as heretofore unknown to me as Bebb was himself. I have no doubt that, as in my earlier novels, I had to do more hard work than I now remember. I had to figure out names for people that seemed to suit them and to explore possible relationships between them. I had to search my memories of the South where they lived so I could get the look and the feel of it more or less right and the country way they some of them had of talking. I had to worry about plot, about what scenes to put in and what scenes to let the readers imagine for themselves. All of that. But in the case of *Lion Country* especially—the first of the four novels I wrote about Bebb —what I found myself involved in was a process much less of invention than of discovery. I had never written a book that seemed so much "on the house." It floated up out of my dreaming so charged with a life of its own that there was a sense in which almost all I had to do was sit back and watch it unfold. Instead of having to force myself to go back to it every morning as I had with novels in the past, I could hardly wait to go back to it; and instead of taking something like two years to write as the earlier ones had, it was all done in just short of three months.

One wonders why. Part of it, I'm sure, was that for the first time as a novelist I used the device of a first-person narrator, and although Antonio Parr was by no means simply myself in thin disguise— our lives had been very different; we had different personalities, different ways of speaking—just to have a person telling his own story in a rather digressive, loose-jointed way was extremely liberating to me as a writer. For the first time I felt free to be funny in ways that I hadn't felt comfortable being in print before, to let some of my saltier-tongued characters use language that before had struck me as less than seemly in a serious work of fiction, to wander off into quirkish reminiscences and observations that weren't always directly related to my central purpose. There was all of that to help make my writer's task an excitement and a delight instead of a burden to labor under, sentence by sentence, scene by scene, until with vast relief I reached the final page at last. But there was also something much more than just that, and what it was, supremely and without any question, was Bebb himself. When I reached the final page of *Lion Country,* I tried my hand at a few other things, but it wasn't long before I started a second novel about him called *Open Heart,* and then *Love Feast,* and then *Treasure Hunt,* none of them ever quite the joy-rides that *Lion Country* had been but all of them written because I couldn't help myself, because I missed Bebb too much to let him go, or because —whatever it may mean to say so—Bebb would not let me go.

What was there about Bebb that engaged me so? Part of what seems to happen in dreams—and what makes them sometimes prophetic—is that in them you live out parts of yourself that have not yet entered your waking life either because you have never consciously recognized them or because for one reason or another you have chosen not to. Earthbound, you dream of flying. Inhibited, you dream of appearing in public stark naked. But it can be subtler than that, more profound and more telling, as dreams open out into the glimmering dusk of modes of being that you have not yet explored and may never explore but which are no less part of the mystery and the poetry of who you are. Bebb appears in the opening scene of *Lion Country* about to head down a flight of subway stairs, and in a way it was down into just such a subterranean dusk that I followed him, except that here I must change the metaphor because where Bebb was, it was rarely dusk. It was dusk, rather, that I left behind in following him.

Where Bebb was, the Florida sunshine was—the hot, bright sun that the lions in the cageless zoo of Lion Country dozed and coupled in, that shone down blindingly on Bebb no less when he did whatever he did in front of the children in Miami Beach than when just possibly he raised his old friend Brownie from the dead in Knoxville, Tennessee. Bebb was strong in most of the places where I was weak, and mad as a hatter in most of the places where I was all too sane. Bebb took terrible risks with his life where I hung back with mine and hoped no one would notice. In more ways than literally, Bebb was continually exposing himself, coming right out and telling it the way it was, let the chips fall where they might, whereas I spent hours by myself every day trying to tell it exactly right and telling other people's stories rather than my own. Bebb's doubts were darker and more painful than mine because he had grown up knowing more of pain and darkness, and that made his faith both a kind of crazy miracle in itself and a faith also that could work miracles.

Life was, above all else, the miracle that Bebb worked, I think, because in one preposterous, Bebbsian way or another he made life burn a little hotter and brighter in all the people who came his way in those four novels and most certainly in myself as well who both brought him into being and was in certain ways, in certain aspects, brought into being with him. He continues, in fact, to be so full of life for me that I find myself inclined to agree at times with his octagenarian friend, Gertrude Conover, that he was no less than a bodhisattva, an always-returner, and, as such, is back to his old tricks again—in me if nowhere else— even though it has been some five years or so since I finished writing about him. I sometimes believe that I can even identify some of his earlier incarnations in my life —as King Rinkitink in one of the Oz books I read as a child, for instance, and as the enormous man who was Thursday in Chesterton's novel, and as the portly and beneficent figure of Tristram Bone, who was the hero of the first novel I wrote myself. Maybe that was why I recognized him so readily when I opened the magazine in the barber shop. Maybe it was by a good deal more than just luck that he floated up into my consciousness that day. Maybe our most life-giving and prophetic dreams are always more than just luck. In any case, it was from Bebb that I learned to be braver about exposing myself and my own story as I have both in this present book and in *The Sacred Journey.* I feel sure that, for better or worse, neither of them could have been written without him.

As a writer I have spent so much time trying to bring my dreams to life that, looking back over the years, I remember occasions when life itself seemed dreamlike by comparison. There was the departure of Katherine and Dinah for boarding school, for instance. I knew perfectly well that they were going. We had driven them around to this school and that school till finally they found the one they liked best. And for the whole summer before they left, there was all the talk about it and all the getting ready for it. And when the day finally came, Judy and I drove them there ourselves and met their roommates and lugged endless bags, boxes, and suitcases up endless flights of stairs for them and kissed them good-bye at last, knowing that in a few weeks we would be seeing them again because the school was in Massachusetts and only a couple of hours away, after all. All of this I knew because I had seen it with my own eyes, but there was one thing that I did not see, and it was the most important thing of all.

What I did not see was that even though they were only a couple of hours away, and even though there would be years of weekends and vacations for us to get together whenever we felt like it, there was a sense in which, when we kissed them good-bye that September afternoon, we were kissing them good-bye for keeps. From that day forward, Vermont would never be home for them again in the way it had been. It would be a place to go for weekends and vacations. From that day forward, home, for them, was theirs to find wherever in themselves or in the world they ever happened to find it, if they were lucky enough to find it at all. Two of the four most precious people in my life had left for good, and I had been looking the other way at the time. Life went on, of course, and I managed to get around much as before, but there were times when it felt like trying to get around on broken legs, and there are times when it feels that way still.

It was not just that I greatly missed them but that I feared for them more greatly still. The world does cruel and hurtful things to us all before it's done with us, and with little more to defend themselves against it than their bags full of clothes and their boxes full of rock records, coat hangers, hockey sticks, it was out into that world that they went. The adventures that they have had since are theirs to tell, not mine, but insofar as from time to time the world has worked them over as it works us all over,

I have suffered vastly more from such pain as they have known than I have ever suffered from any pain simply of my own. As Buddha well knew, that is the price that love exacts from us all, but since from childhood I have always been given to helpless brooding and worrying and darkest, most doom-ridden imagining, the price it has exacted from me has often proved crippling both to myself and to the ones I love.

Love is a key concept in Buddhism and Christianity both, needless to say. Buddhism, in the long run, seems to come out against it except in the sense of something like *upekha,* which is a love so vast and passionless, so disembodied and impartial, that it ceases to resemble the Christian form in any very apparent way. Buddhism comes out against it not just for one's own sake in the sense that to love another is to open the door into a whole new realm of vulnerability and suffering for oneself, but for the sake of the other also in the sense that unless we can break all the fetters, including love, which bind us to the wheel of rebirth, we can never achieve that Nirvana-like state of selfless detachment which is the only state in which we can be of any real use toward helping others to achieve it. Bloodless, remote, and mythical as these Buddhist insights are apt to seem from a Christian perspective, they are nonetheless greatly useful, I think, in deepening our understanding of love in a Christian sense.

That to love other people is to suffer when they suffer is a truth of life which Christianity recognizes no less than Buddhism does. It is a truth which has much to do, of course, with what the Cross is all about. To say that Christ takes upon himself the sins of the world is to say that he takes upon himself the suffering of the world too. It is to say that in a sense his suffering on the Cross continues for as long as any of us suffers. Furthermore, in being called to take up our own crosses and follow him, we are called to participate in his suffering. But unlike Buddhism, Christianity nevertheless affirms this love that suffers and, what is more, affirms it not in spite of the fact that it suffers but because of it. It affirms it for the reason that to love others to the point of suffering with them and for them in their own suffering is the only way ultimately to heal them, redeem them, if they are to be redeemed at all. It is God's way in Christ, and as we are called to participate with Christ in his suffering, so we are called to be partners with him in his work of redemption. For our own sakes as well as for theirs, we are called to be Christs to all humankind, in other words, and that is close to the heart of our faith and of our lives together as Christians.

And yet. And yet. Having spoken this Christian truth, we must also, I think, remember the Buddhist truth which may be closer to it than at first glance it appears. If love is a matter of holding fast to, and identifying with, and suffering for, the ones we love, it is a matter also of standing back from, of leaving space for, of letting go of. To become, through loving and needing them, as involved in the lives of others as I was involved in the lives of my children is in the long run to risk being both crippled and crippling. Because we love our children as helplessly as we do, they have the power to destroy us. We must not let them, for their own sakes no less than for our own. A distance must be kept—not just from our children but from everyone we love. I think of the Buddha sitting under his Bo-tree with his eyes closed upon an inner peace which he would not permit even his great compassion to disturb. I think of the staff of the East Harlem Protestant Parish with the pale northern blue of their compassion, their sad gaiety, their utter lack of sentimentality. I think of Jesus himself, who in the profoundest sense bled for people but was never what is meant by "a bleeding heart"; who did what he could for the sick and suffering who came his way and then moved on; who wept for Jerusalem but let Jerusalem choose its own way; who kept his own mother at arm's length and, when Mary Magdalen reached out to embrace him at the end, said, "Do not touch me."

We are to love one another as God has loved us. That is the truth of it. But to love one another more than God has loved us—to love one another at the expense of our own freedom to be something like whole and at peace within ourselves, and at the expense of others' freedom, too —is the dark shadow that the truth casts. This is what I started to learn when Katherine and Dinah went away to school in 1975 and launched forth on lives of their own. What event could have been less earthshaking? Yet for me it shook the very foundations themselves and marked the beginning of a new leg of the journey which I am in the midst of still.

It is this new leg of the journey that the last novel I wrote is about, I suppose, although I don't believe I thought of it that way at the time. *Godric* is what I called it because the tale it tells is of an English saint by that name, a man who was born the year before the Norman Conquest and died in 1170 at the age of one hundred and five by the river Wear, near Durham, where he had lived as a hermit for the last sixty years of his life. Like Bebb, he came to me by accident, if there are such things as accidents in matters like this. Do our dreams come by accident? I was sitting not in a barber shop this time but in the room at home where I work these days. I picked up a small paperback book of saints and opened it, by accident, to the page that had Godric on it. I had never so much as heard of him before, but as I read about him, I knew he was for me, my saint. He had been a peddler before he turned hermit, and master of a merchant ship. He had tried his hand at piracy for a while. He had rescued Baldwin the First, King of Jerusalem, at the time of the First Crusade. He had not considered himself a saint at all and for that reason balked at giving his blessing to the excessively reverent biography that a contemporary monk called Reginald of Durham was writing about him. Maybe Godric was actually Bebb in an earlier incarnation, I thought for a time, but though it was a notion that helped get me started, I soon dropped it.

Godric came as mysteriously alive for me as Bebb had and, with him, all the people he knew and the whole medieval world he lived in. I had Godric narrate his own life, and despite the problem of developing a language that sounded authentic on his lips without becoming impenetrably archaic, and despite the difficulties of trying to recapture a time and place so unlike my own, the book, like *Lion Country* before it, came so quickly and with such comparative ease that there were times when I suspected that maybe the old saint himself was not entirely uninvolved in the process, as, were I a saint and were somebody writing a book about me, I would not be entirely uninvolved in the process either.

All sorts of adventures are described in the book because Godric's life was full of adventures, and I followed his life as accurately as I could; but Godric is a very old man as he tells his tale, and old age and the approach of death are very much in the back of his mind throughout. In this sense I think it was a book as prophetic, for me, as the Bebb books had been. It was prophetic in the sense that in its pages, more than half without knowing it, I was trying on various ways of growing old and facing death myself. As the years go by, Godric outlives, or is left behind by, virtually everybody he has ever loved—his sister, Burcwen; his shipmate, Roger Mouse; the two snakes, Tune and Fairweather, who for years were his constant companions; and the beautiful maid, Gillian, who appeared to him on the way back from his pilgrimage to Rome. But, although not without anguish, he is able to let them all go finally and to survive their going. His humanity and wit survive. His faith survives. He prays. He sins. He dreams. And one day not long before his death bathing in the icy waters of the river Wear as for years he has bathed there, summer and winter, to chasten his flesh he feels his arms and legs go numb, his pulse all but stop, and speaks these words both for himself and also for me:

> "Praise, praise!" I croak. Praise God for all that's holy, cold, and dark. Praise him for all we lose, for all the river of the years bears off. Praise him for stillness in the wake of pain. Praise him for emptiness. And as you race to spill into the sea, praise him yourself, old Wear. Praise him for dying and the peace of death.[26]

If I should live to be one hundred and five myself, I have almost half my journey still ahead of me. I do not know what adventures I will have along the way or what new sights may await me around the next bend, and not knowing is fine by me. There are times when I suspect the world may come to an end before most of us are ready to—which would have the advantage at least of our not having to leave, one by one, while the party is still going strong—but most of the time I believe that the world will manage somehow to survive us, and that has its advantages too. I suppose Judy and I will keep on living in Vermont because after all these years it's hard to imagine living anywhere else, and as long as the dreams keep being dreamed, I suppose I will go on writing books. They never reach as wide a public as I would like—too religious for secular readers, I suspect, and too secular for religious ones—but in the end justice is almost always done in literary matters, I believe, and if they are worth enduring, they will endure. Who can say? Humanly speaking, in fact, who can say for sure about anything? And yet there are some things I would be willing to bet maybe even my life on.

That life is grace, for instance—the givenness of it, the fathomlessness of it, the endless possibilities of its becoming transparent to something extraordinary beyond itself. That—as I picked up somewhere in Jung and whittled into the ash stick I use for tramping around through the woods sometimes—*vocatus atque non vocatus Deus aderit,* which I take to mean that in the long run, whether you call on him or don't call on him, God will be present with you. That if we really had our eyes open, we would see that all moments are key moments. That he who does not love remains in death. That Jesus is the Word made flesh who dwells among us full of grace and truth. On good days I might add a few more to the list. On bad days it's possible there might be a few less.

Beyond that, all I can do with real assurance is once more to echo my old teacher Paul Tillich to the effect that here and there even in our world, and now and then even in ourselves, we catch glimpses of a New Creation, which, fleeting as those glimpses are apt to be, give us hope both for this life and for whatever life may await us later on.

"What's lost is nothing to what's found," as Godric says, "and all the death that ever was, set next to life, would scarcely fill a cup."[27]

Notes

1. Eleanor Ruggles, *Gerard Manley Hopkins* (New York: W. W. Norton & Co., 1944), p. 98.
2. Paul Tillich, *The New Being* (New York: Charles Scribner's Sons, 1955), pp. 17–18 *passim.*
3. Annie Dillard, *Holy the Firm* (New York: Harper & Row, 1977), p. 59.
4. Genesis 27:27.
5. Gerard Manley Hopkins, "Felix Randal," *The Poems of Gerard Manley Hopkins* (London: Oxford University Press, 1967), p. 86.
6. Mark 10:17ff.
7. John Donne, "The Relique," *The Poems of John Donne* (London: Oxford University Press, 1938), p. 62.
8. Frederick Buechner, *The Return of Ansel Gibbs* (New York: Alfred Knopf, 1958), pp. 40–41.
9. Walter Kaufman, ed., *Existentialism from Dostoyevsky to Sartre* (New York: Meridian Books, 1956), pp. 294–5.
10. Albert Camus, *The Myth of Sisyphus* (New York: Vintage Books, 1959), p. 44.
11. Søren Kierkegaard, *Selections from the Writings of Søren Kierkegaard* (New York: Anchor Books, 1960), p. 150.
12. Philippians 2:7–8.
13. Ephesians 4:13.
14. John B. Noss, *Man's Religions* (New York: Macmillan Co., 1957), p. 173.
15. John 15:12.

16. Ernest Hemingway, *A Farewell to Arms* (New York: Charles Scribner's Sons, 1929), p. 267.
17. 1 John 3:18.
18. Graham Greene, *The Power and the Glory* (New York: Viking Press, 1940), p. 112.
19. Frederick Buechner, *The Final Beast* (New York: Atheneum, 1965), p. 182 *passim*.
20. Mark 9:24.
21. Karl Barth, *The Word of God and the Word of Man* (New York: Harper & Bros., 1957), pp. 125–26.
22. Ibid., p. 105.
23. Ibid., p. 105.
24. Ibid., p. 108.
25. Ibid., p. 117.
26. Frederick Buechner, *Godric* (New York: Atheneum, 1980), p. 96.
27. Ibid.